Desires of the Heart

Prayers for Growing Faith

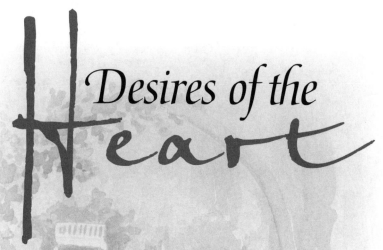

Desires of the Heart

Prayers for Growing Faith

Bill Huebsch,
with Leisa Anslinger

TWENTY THIRD 23rd
PUBLICATIONS

Twenty-Third Publications
A Division of Bayard
One Montauk Avenue, Suite 200
New London, CT 06320
(860) 437-3012 or (800) 321-0411
www.23rdpublications.com
ISBN 10: 1-58595-556-6
ISBN 978-1-58595-556-5

Contents

Introduction 1

BOOKLET 1 Our Hearts Desire God 3

BOOKLET 2 God's Loving Plan 6

BOOKLET 3 The Church Hands On God's Revelation 9

BOOKLET 4 God Speaks through Scripture 12

BOOKLET 5 Our Response of Faith 15

BOOKLET 6 I Believe in God 18

BOOKLET 7 The Love of the Trinity 21

BOOKLET 8 God Created the World 24

BOOKLET 9 We Are Made in God's Image 27

BOOKLET 10 Turning Back to God 30

BOOKLET 11 Jesus Is the Messiah! 33

BOOKLET 12 Mary, God's Mother and Ours 36

BOOKLET 13 Christ Taught about the Kingdom 39

BOOKLET 14 Jesus Died that We Might Live 42

BOOKLET 15 Encounter the Risen Christ 45

BOOKLET 16 The Holy Spirit Enflames Hearts 48

BOOKLET 17 The Mystery of the Church 51

BOOKLET 18 Characteristics of the Church 54

BOOKLET 19 We Are the Church 57

BOOKLET 20 The Communion of Saints 60

BOOKLET 21 Liturgy: Source of Our Lives 63

BOOKLET 22 Celebrating the Liturgy 66

BOOKLET 23 Baptism: Birth into New Life 69

BOOKLET 24 Confirmation: Gift of the Spirit 72

BOOKLET 25	Eucharist: the Bread of Life	75
BOOKLET 26	God Offers Unending Forgiveness	78
BOOKLET 27	God Heals Us through Anointing	81
BOOKLET 28	Consecrated for Service	84
BOOKLET 29	Love Blessed and Celebrated	87
BOOKLET 30	Free in the Spirit	90
BOOKLET 31	Making Moral Judgments	93
BOOKLET 32	The Greatest Virtue Is Love	96
BOOKLET 33	Turning Away from God	99
BOOKLET 34	Living as a Community	102
BOOKLET 35	Sharing God's Life	105
BOOKLET 36	Living with the Mind of Christ	108
BOOKLET 37	We Worship One God	111
BOOKLET 38	We Keep Holy the Lord's Day	114
BOOKLET 39	Forming a Household of Faith	117
BOOKLET 40	Protecting Human Life	120
BOOKLET 41	Called to Chastity	123
BOOKLET 42	Generosity of Heart	126
BOOKLET 43	The Truth Makes Us Free	129
BOOKLET 44	Our Relationship with God	132
BOOKLET 45	Jesus Teaches Us to Pray	135
BOOKLET 46	God Speaks to Us in Prayer	138
BOOKLET 47	Becoming Persons of Prayer	141
BOOKLET 48	The Lord's Prayer	144

Introduction

What does *your* heart desire?
The human heart is filled with hunger.
No matter who we are or where we live,
    no matter how rich or poor we've become,
    no matter if we're married or single,
        no matter what,
            we hunger.
And for what is it that we humans hunger?
When we pause to consider this
    in all its magnitude and power,
    we realize that we hunger for that One who made us.
        We hunger for the divine heart.
        We hunger for God.
This desire for God is written into our very hearts,
    because we are created by God and for God
        and God never ceases to draw us to God's own self.

"Only in God will we ever find the truth and happiness
    for which we never stop searching."

So begins article 26 of the *Catechism of the Catholic Church*, as present-ed in booklet 1 of the *Growing Faith Project*. Indeed, we humans are filled with a longing that can only be satisfied by our immersion in the life imagined and intended for us by God. From the very beginning, having been made in God's image and likeness, we have been destined to desire this. We long for the One who made us. We long for the One who continues to make us more whole every day of our lives.

    This book of prayers is meant to be used as a companion to the sys-tematic study you are doing through the series of booklets known as *The Growing Faith Project*. This project offers you the entire spectrum of Catholic teaching as presented in the official catechism of the

Church, but it does so in plain, poetic language that lifts the heart and soul. As you study these booklets, sharing faith with others and growing in faith yourself, pause now and then to use this prayer resource. Let these prayers connect you to that One in whom you believe, that one God who is found within your heart.

These prayers may be used as part of your own private devotion, or they may be used in a group with others who are on the same journey. These others—fellow parishioners, family members, friends, coworkers in God's vineyard—all share the one faith that is growing within you. Together, you will grow even more firmly to believe and understand your faith. Let this resource be a strong blessing for you. Let it nourish you.

Each prayer within this book is designed to match one of the Growing Faith booklets. Within each prayer, simple instructions will guide you

    to pause
    to listen to sacred music
    to reflect on Scripture
    to ask deep questions
    to share your thoughts or reflect alone
    and to commit yourself to action.

Take your time as you pray; do not rush God's spirit as it flows through you. Allow your heart to be touched, and pay attention to intuitions and divine inspiration as it emerges within you. Be guided by God's own hand as you study and live your faith.

We who are the editors and writers of this prayer book
    send you our own blessing.
We hope you will become a strong person of purpose,
    a person who follows the way of God,
    a person who lives what you believe.
May God's own hand be upon you;
    may you know the peace of Christ,
    may you grow daily in faith,
    and may you touch others with profound love. Amen.

Our Hearts Desire God

"How can your soul find rest, except for the Lord?"

Relax and center your mind and heart in God's presence. Let your whole being enter into prayer.

Invitation to Pray

Our God is the God of light and life. Thanks be to God for the wonder of God's mystery! Turn your heart now to God, and begin in the name of the Father, and of the Son, and of the Holy Spirit. Amen.

Prepare Your Heart

We all have an inborn hunger for God. Pause for a moment to reflect: How do you experience this hunger? What word(s) could you use to express this hunger?

If you are with others, share your reflections if you are comfortable doing so. If you are alone, reflect silently.

The Word of God

For from the greatness and beauty of created things comes a corresponding perception of their Creator. Yet these people are little to be blamed, for perhaps they go astray while seeking God and desiring to find him. For while they live among his works, they keep searching, and they trust in what they see, because the things that are seen are beautiful. Yet again, not even they are to be excused; for if they had the power to know so much that they could investigate the world, how did they fail to find sooner the Lord of these things? (Wis 13:5–9)

Reflection

If you are with others, share your reflections on these questions insofar as you are comfortable doing so. If you are alone, pause to reflect in silence, then write some notes in the space provided.

► For what or whom do you thirst?

► What is of greatest value to you in your life?

► How do you experience weariness? What revives your spirit?

Meditation on Music

Allow a moment or two of silence to fill your prayer space, then listen to or sing along with "Come to the Water" by John Foley, SJ (track 1 on CD).

O let all who thirst, let them come to the water.
And let all who have nothing, let them come to the Lord:
Without money, without price.
Why should you pay the price, except for the Lord?

And let all who toil, let them come to the water.
And let all who are weary, let them come to the Lord:
All who labor, without rest.
How can your soul find rest, except for the Lord.

Prayer

O loving God, in our hearts we desire you above all things.
  Hear our prayer and bless all those who hunger for your love.

Pause and reflect on Jesus' call to love one another.

We pray for all who seek you, for the lost, the poor, and the weak,
  for the sick, the dying, and those who care for them,
  for those who need strength in the face of doubt or trial.

Pause and recall the times when you most feel the hunger and need for God's love.

Lord Jesus, who spoke to the Samaritan woman
  of the thirst for living water,
  keep that thirst for God alive in our hearts.
May you remain in our hearts and be our life,
  especially in the lonely and difficult moments.
O God, bless us and keep us, now and always. Amen.

Actions

• Resolve to share words of hope with someone in pain.

• Commit yourself to pausing for at least a few moments each day for silent prayer.

Close

End your prayer by listening quietly one more time to the song "Come to the Water."

God's Loving Plan

"I call your name."

Relax and center your mind and heart in God's presence. Let your whole being enter into prayer.

Invitation to Pray

Let us turn our hearts to God in Christ, and give thanks for the times during the day when we encounter God. Begin in the name of the Father, and of the Son, and of the Holy Spirit. Amen.

Prepare Your Heart

God communicates God's own self to us. How do you understand this to happen? How do you recognize God's presence in your life?

If you are with others, share your reflections with them if you are comfortable doing so. If you are alone, pause and reflect in silence.

The Word of God

The days are surely coming, says the Lord, when I will make a new covenant with the house of Israel and the house of Judah….I will put my law within them, and I will write it on their hearts; and I will be their God, and they shall be my people. No longer shall they teach one another, or say to each other, "Know the Lord," for they shall all know me, from the least of them to the greatest, says the Lord; for I will forgive their iniquity, and remember their sin no more. (Jer 31:31–34)

REFLECTION

If you are with others, share your reflections with them if you are comfortable doing so. If you are alone, pause and reflect in silence, then write notes in the space provided.

▶ How does God comfort you?

▶ How might God be calling you to live more authentically as a person of faith?

▶ At this time in your life, how are you called to trust in God's providence?

MEDITATION ON MUSIC

Allow a moment or two of silence, then listen to or sing along with "Turn to Me" by John Foley, SJ (track 2 on CD).

Turn to me, O turn, and be saved,
says the Lord, for I am God;
there is no other, none beside me.
I call your name.

I am God, who comforts you;
who are you to be afraid of flesh that fades,
is made like the grass of the field, soon to wither.

Listen to me, my people; give ear to me, my nation:
a law will go forth from me,
and my justice for a light to the people.

Text based on Isaiah 45:22-23; 51:12, 4, 6. Text and music © 1975, John B. Foley, SJ and OCP Publications. All rights reserved.

Prayer

When we turn our backs on your presence in other people,
  when we treat others with indifference and neglect,
    and even when we need your strength to "go the extra mile"
    show us the way of conversion.
Let your Spirit kindle the flame of love in us,
  and give us the sensitivity to discover your presence.

Pause to recall those times when you most need the Spirit's guidance in being aware of others.

We bring in prayer the needs of your people, O God:
  the Church, which is called to be a sign of Christ's love,
  those who cry for mercy and justice,
  all who rely on God in the face of violence,
  those who bear Christ's light through sacrifice,
  all who most need God's care.

Pause to pray for the gift of awareness.

Help us always see your presence in our sisters and brothers,
  and serve them as we would serve you.
Christ, sacrament of the Father,
  we see the presence of God in the Eucharist,
  in the people with whom we worship at the Sunday assembly.
Give us a spirit of reverence
  as we live out our daily lives. Amen.

Actions

• Listen to the prophets of today who are calling us to bring about change, and do what you can, no matter how small the action.

• Be more aware of God's presence during the celebration of the Eucharist.

Close

End your prayer by listening quietly again to the song "Turn to Me."

The Church Hands On God's Revelation

*"Brothers and sisters, each of us called
to walk in your light."*

*Relax and focus your mind and heart on God's presence. Let your whole
being enter into prayer.*

Invitation to Pray

Christ is the light of the world; the Spirit of truth guides us! Open
your heart to God, and begin in the name of the Father, and of the
Son, and of the Holy Spirit. Amen.

Prepare Your Heart

When we hear the word proclaimed, we hear the voice of God. How
has God's word, Jesus Christ, touched and guided your life?

*If you are with others, you may share your reflections if you wish. If you
are alone, reflect in silence.*

The Word of God

In the beginning was the Word, and the Word was with God, and the
Word was God. He was in the beginning with God. All things came
into being through him, and without him not one thing came into

being. What has come into being in him was life, and the life was the light of all people. The light shines in the darkness, and the darkness did not overcome it. (Jn 1:1–5)

REFLECTION

If you are with others, share your reflections if you wish. If you are alone, reflect in silence, then write notes in the space provided.

▶ How does the Spirit guide you to the truth?

▶ Is there some part of your heart that needs to be freed? What is it?

▶ In what areas of your life do you need God's mercy and hope?

MEDITATION ON MUSIC

Remain in silence for a moment or two, then listen to or sing along with "Gather Your People" by Bob Hurd (track 3 on CD).

Gather your people, O Lord.
Gather your people, O Lord.
One bread, one body, one spirit of love.
Gather your people, O Lord.

Draw us forth to the table of life: brothers and sisters,
each of us called to walk in your light.

We are parts of the body of Christ, needing each other,
each of the gifts the Spirit provides.

Text: Based on 1 Corinthians 12; Isaiah 2:3-4, 11:9. Text and music © 1991, Bob Hurd. Published by OCP Publications. All rights reserved.

Prayer

O God of goodness and generosity,
  we come to you in prayer.
In you we place our confidence,
  not trusting in our strength.
Fill us with your love, all-loving God!

Pause and reflect on the needs of the Church.

Look down on us your Church,
  and send the light of grace!
Guide us in our decisions,
  send guidance to your Church.
Be love! O guiding Spirit,
  hear now our holy prayers.
We share one faith and love.

Actions

• Ask yourself in what way you can minister to the people of the Church, today.

• Pause to listen to the Spirit speaking to you through the events of your day.

Close

End your prayer by listening quietly one more time to the song "Gather Your People."

God Speaks through Scripture

"Your words are spirit and life."

Relax and center your mind and heart in God's presence. Let your whole being enter into prayer.

Invitation to Pray

We live by faith and are formed by God's word. We make the sign of our faith, and begin in the name of the Father, and of the Son, and of the Holy Spirit. Amen.

Prepare Your Heart

The Bible is a "library of books." Which book speaks most to you at this point in your life? Why?

If you are with others, share your reflections if you wish. If you are alone, reflect in silence.

The Word of God

Then Jesus said to his disciples, "These are my words that I spoke to you while I was still with you—that everything written about me in the law of Moses, the prophets, and the psalms must be fulfilled." Then he opened their minds to understand the scriptures, and he said to them, "Thus it is written, that the Messiah is to suffer and to rise from the dead on the third day, and that repentance and forgiveness of sins is to be proclaimed in his name to all nations, beginning in Jerusalem. You are witnesses of these things. And see, I am sending

upon you what my Father promised; so stay here in the city until you
have been clothed with power from on high." (Lk 24:44–49)

Reflection

If you are with others, share your reflections if you wish. If alone, reflect in silence, then write notes in the space provided.

▶ How do you find God's wisdom within sacred Scripture?

▶ Recall a time in your life when the word of God gave you new vision. How did this happen? What did you learn?

▶ How did your life change as a result?

Meditation on Music

Pause in prayerful silence for a moment or two, then listen to or sing along with "Your Words Are Spirit and Life" by Bernadette Farrell (track 4 on CD).

Your words are spirit and life, O Lord:
richer than gold, stronger than death.
Your words are spirit and life, O Lord; life everlasting.

God's precepts keep us; their purpose is right.
They gladden the hearts of people.
God's command is so clear it brings us new vision;
bringing God's light to our eyes.

Living by God's truth is holy and sure;
God's presence is everlasting.
God's truth is eternal, bringing us justice;
bringing God's justice to earth.

Text: Based on Psalm 19:8-11. Text and music © 1993, Bernadette Farrell. Published by OCP
Publications. All rights reserved.

Prayer

O Spirit of God, be with us as we pray.
We stand here before you,
> longing for you,
> bound to love one another.

Abide, O Spirit of life!

Brief sacred pause
Let peace fill our hearts,
> let love fill our minds.

Make us loving disciples of Christ.
May we all be one,
> may we all be yours,

Abide, O Spirit of Life!

Pause to remember those situations in which you need to act with justice, and pray for those who need it most.

We ask you to guide all our actions
> and to show the path we should walk.

We desire to know what will please you.
Abide, O Spirit of Life!

Actions

• Resolve to make time to read the Bible as a personal message to you.

• Apply the Scripture that you read to your everyday life.

Close

End your prayer by listening quietly one more time to the song "Your Words Are Spirit and Life."

Our Response of Faith

"I have called you and you are mine."

Relax and focus your mind and heart on God. Let your whole being enter into prayer.

Invitation to Pray

Blessed are we, beloved of God! Turn your heart now to God and begin in the name of the Father, and of the Son, and of the Holy Spirit. Amen.

Prepare Your Heart

Faith enlightens us, helping us see truth. What does your faith help you see?

If you are with others, share your reflections if you wish. If alone, reflect in silence.

The Word of God

By faith Abraham obeyed when he was called to set out for a place that he was to receive as an inheritance; and he set out, not knowing where he was going. By faith he stayed for a time in the land he had been promised, as in a foreign land, living in tents, as did Isaac and Jacob, who were heirs with him of the same promise. For he looked forward to the city that has foundations, whose architect and builder is God. By faith he received power of procreation, even though he was too old—and Sarah herself was barren—because he considered him faithful who had promised. Therefore from one person, and this one as good as dead, descendants were born, "as many as the stars of heaven and the innumerable grains of sand by the seashore." (Heb 11:8–12)

REFLECTION

If you are with others, share your reflections if you wish. If alone, reflect in silence, then write notes in the space provided.

▶ How does God meet your longing with love?

▶ How do you experience joy and hope in Christ?

▶ Into what darkness does Christ's light shine in your life?

MEDITATION ON MUSIC

Allow a moment or two of prayerful silence, then listen to or sing along with "I Have Loved You" by Michael Joncas (track 5 on CD).

I have loved you with an everlasting love,
I have called you and you are mine;
I have loved you with an everlasting love,
I have called you and you are mine.

Seek the face of the Lord and long for him:
he will bring you his light and his peace.

Text based on Jeremiah 31:3; Psalm 24:3. Text and music © 1979, OCP Publications. All rights reserved.

PRAYER

O loving God, we place our faith and trust in you,
    asking for the light of your Spirit.
Hear our prayers and keep us close to you.

Brief sacred pause

We pray for these gifts, O God, for ourselves
  and for our sisters and brothers in faith:
  for the gift of faith,
  for understanding of others,
  for simplicity of spirit,
  for a heart that trusts in God,
  for all who struggle to believe.

Pause and recall the gifts God has blessed us with, and give God praise.

Blessed be the Lord God of Israel
  for he has looked favorably on
  his people and redeemed them.
He has raised up a mighty savior for us
  in the house of his servant David.
Thus he has shown the mercy
  promised to our ancestors,
  and has remembered his holy covenant.
By the tender mercy of our God
  the dawn from on high will break upon us,
  to give light to those in darkness
  and in the shadow of death,
  to guide our feet into the way of peace. Amen.

(Lk 1:68–79)

Actions

• Mary embodies what it means to have faith. Imitate her loving "yes" when you are asked to do something for God this week.

• Pass on the faith through a word or action, no matter how small.

Close

End your prayer by listening quietly one more time to the song "I Have Loved You."

I Believe in God

"All that breathes, bless the Lord."

Relax and center your mind and heart in God. Let your whole being enter into prayer.

Invitation to Pray

We lift our hearts to God who promises to love us. Turn to God now with trust and begin in the name of the Father, and of the Son, and of the Holy Spirit. Amen.

Prepare Your Heart

We are assured that even if the mountains fall, God will remain with us. How do you respond to this amazing promise?

If you are with others, share your reflections if you wish. If alone, reflect in silence.

The Word of God

There the angel of the Lord appeared to Moses in a flame of fire out of a bush; he looked, and the bush was blazing, yet it was not consumed. Then Moses said, "I must turn aside and look at this great sight, and see why the bush is not burned up." When the Lord saw that he had turned aside to see, God called to him out of the bush, "Moses, Moses!" And he said, "Here I am." Then he said, "Come no closer! Remove the sandals from your feet, for the place on which you are standing is holy ground."

Moses said to God, "If I come to the Israelites and say to them, 'The God of your ancestors has sent me to you,' and they ask me, 'What is his name?' what shall I say to them?" God said to Moses, "I am who I am." (Ex 3:2–6, 13–14a)

Reflection

If you are with others, share your reflections if you wish. If alone, reflect in silence, then write notes in the space provided.

▶ Do you experience God's love as that of a parent for a child? Or as a spouse for his or her beloved? Explain.

▶ How do you "abide in love" and "abide in God"?

Meditation on Music

Allow a moment or two of prayerful silence, then listen to or sing along with "We Will Praise You" by Tom Kendzia (track 6 on CD).

We will praise you with the sun and the moon,
with the sea and all that it holds.
Earth and heaven sing the glory of God,
all creation praises your name.

O my soul, bless the Lord;
all that lives, bless the Lord.
Praise your name above all names;
all that breathes, bless the Lord.

You trees that grow, the winter snow,
you works of God, bless the Lord.
The winds that howl, the thunder's growl,
sing the power of your name.

Prayer

O God, you are love and truth.
> You are also a mystery beyond words.

Faith leads us to desire only you.
Accept what is in our hearts
> and keep us close to you.

Brief sacred pause

We bring to you our needs
> and those of all your children.

We pray for open hearts and minds in all,
> for understanding that leads to compassion based on Christ's love,
> for those who feel far from God's eternal love,
> for all who seek the truth,
> for all who need God's care.

Pause to recall that God does not deceive, for God is truth itself. Pray for those who would lead others astray.

Lord God,
> change the hearts of those who would lead astray
> your faithful people through false ideas
> and the lure of power and wealth.

May they see that you are the true
> and everlasting Good.

May they find the path to you. Amen.

Actions

- What are your names for God? Compose a prayer using them.
- Take some action, no matter how small, against the idols of wealth, power, ideologies.

Close

End your prayer by listening quietly one more time to the song "We Will Praise You."

The Love of the Trinity

"Safe in your hands, all creation is made new."

Relax and center your mind and heart in God. Let your whole being enter into prayer.

Invitation to Pray

We are aware that God is always with us. Turn your heart toward our loving God and begin in the name of the Father, and of the Son, and of the Holy Spirit. Amen.

Prepare Your Heart

Blessed Elizabeth of the Trinity said, "Make [my soul] your heaven, your beloved dwelling." How do you perceive God, Father, Son, and Spirit, dwelling within you?

If you are with others, share your reflections if you wish. If alone, reflect in silence.

The Word of God

If you love me, you will keep my commandments. And I will ask the Father, and he will give you another Advocate, to be with you forever. This is the Spirit of truth, whom the world cannot receive, because it neither sees him nor knows him. You know him, because he abides with you, and he will be in you. I will not leave you orphaned; I am coming to you. In a little while the world will no longer see me, but you will see me; because I live, you also will live. On that day you will know that I am in my Father, and you in me, and I in you. (Jn 14:15–20)

Reflection

If you are with others, share your reflections if you wish. If alone, reflect in silence, then write notes in the space provided.

▶ How do you recognize that God has been with you, in your past and in your present?

▶ How are you sure of safety in God's hands?

▶ How is your life a reflection of the love of the Father? the Son? the Spirit?

Meditation on Music

Allow a moment or two of prayerful silence, then listen to or sing along with "O God, You Search Me" by Bernadette Farrell (track 7 on CD).

O God, you search me and you know me.
All my thoughts lie open to your gaze.
When I walk or lie down you are before me:
Ever the maker and keeper of my days.

For you created me and shaped me,
Gave me life within my mother's womb.
For the wonder of who I am, I praise you:
Safe in your hands, all creation is made new.

Prayer

Be love! Almighty God!
In you we place our confidence,
    not trusting in our strength.
Be love! All loving God!
Look down on us your Church,
    and send the light of grace!

Be love! O Holy Spirit,
Guide us in our decisions,
    send order to your Church.
Be love! O guiding Spirit,
    hear now our holy prayers.
We share one faith and love.

*Pause and recall the times when you saw the love of the Trinity, Father,
Son, and Spirit in our world, and thank God.*

Be love! O God of all creation,
    make all things come out well
    and be with us forever.
Be love! O blessed Spirit,
    who gives us your gifts
    of holiness and grace.
Be love! O Jesus Christ,
    you save us from all harm
    and lead us to salvation.

Actions

• Actively work to bring about a community of love in your Church
and neighborhood.

• Celebrate the Eucharist with more awareness of the action of the
Trinity in you and in the assembly.

Close

End your prayer by listening quietly one more time to the song "O
God, You Search Me."

God Created the World

*"God, beyond all words,
all creation tells your story."*

*Relax and center your mind and heart in God. Let your whole being enter
into prayer.*

Invitation to Pray

God is the creator of all and sustains all in perfect love. We lift our
hearts to God and begin in the name of the Father, and of the Son,
and of the Holy Spirit. Amen.

Prepare Your Heart

You cannot prove there is a God with scientific instruments. How do
you know God exists?

*If you are with others, share your reflections if you wish. If alone, reflect
in silence.*

The Word of God

You stretch out the heavens like a tent,
    you set the beams of your chambers on the waters,
    you make the clouds your chariot,
    you ride on the wings of the wind,
    you make the winds your messengers,
    fire and flame your ministers.

You set the earth on its foundations,
 so that it shall never be shaken.
You cover it with the deep as with a garment;
 the waters stood above the mountains.
They rose up to the mountains, ran down to the valleys
 to the place that you appointed for them.
You set a boundary that they may not pass,
 so that they might not again cover the earth. (Ps 104:2–7, 8–9)

REFLECTION

If you are with others, share your reflections if you wish. If alone, reflect in silence, then write notes in the space provided.

▶ How does recognition that you are created in God's image challenge or shape your self-perception?

▶ Does your interaction with the environment evidence your understanding that everything is created by God?

MEDITATION ON MUSIC

Allow a moment or two for prayerful silence, then listen to or sing along with "God, Beyond All Names" by Bernadette Farrell (track 8 on CD).

God, beyond all names, you have made us in your image;
we are like you, we reflect you; we are woman, we are man.

All around us we have known you, all creation lives to hold you.
In our living and our dying we are bringing you to birth.

God, beyond all words, all creation tells your story;
you have shaken with our laughter,
you have trembled with our tears.

Prayer

United in love,
   we bring our prayers to you, creator God.
Bless our footsteps
   as we journey together with you.

Brief sacred pause

Loving, powerful God, we desire
   the wisdom to be good stewards of creation,
   the strength to avoid all that is evil,
   and a spirit of sharing with those who are in need.

Recall the moments when you could have reached out to another and did not. Ask forgiveness.

Merciful God,
I have not always been as generous
   as you call me to be.
I have not always seen your face in others.
Too often I have been careless and wasteful of
   the goods of creation.
Give me the wisdom and strength to change my ways. Amen.

Actions

• Take a step to correct an injustice or to protect the environment.

• Read and reflect on one of the accounts of creation in Scripture: Genesis 1:1—2:4 or Genesis 2:5–25.

Close

End your prayer by listening quietly once again to the song "God, Beyond All Names."

We Are Made in God's Image

"All creation praises your name."

Relax and focus your mind and heart on God. Let your whole being enter into prayer.

Invitation to Pray

We praise God, in whose image we are created. Turn your minds and hearts to God and begin in the name of the Father, and of the Son, and of the Holy Spirit. Amen.

Prepare Your Heart

We are created to partner with the earth itself, to share its resources and live in gratitude. How do you think we humans are doing? What are you doing personally in this regard?

If you are with others, share your reflections if you wish. If alone, reflect in silence.

The Word of God.

Then God said, "Let us make humankind in our image, according to our likeness; and let them have dominion over the fish of the sea, and over the birds of the air, and over the cattle, and over all the wild animals of the earth, and over every creeping thing that creeps upon the earth." So God created humankind in his image, in the image of God he created them; male and female he created them. God blessed them, and God said to them, "Be fertile and multiply, and fill the earth and subdue it; and have dominion over the fish of the sea and over the birds of the air and over every living thing that moves upon the earth." God said, "See, I have given you every plant yielding seed that is upon the face of all the earth, and every tree with seed in its fruit; you shall have them for food. And to every beast of the earth, and to every bird of the air, and to everything that creeps on the earth, everything that has the breath of life, I have given every green plant for food." And it was so. God saw everything that he had made, and indeed, it was very good. (Gen 1:26–31)

Reflection

If you are with others, share your reflections if you wish. If alone, reflect in silence, then write notes in the space provided.

▶ What does it mean to you to be created in God's image? How does mindfulness of that image guide you in your choices?

Meditation on Music

Allow a moment or two for prayerful silence, then listen to or sing along with "We Will Praise You" by Tom Kendzia (track 6 on CD).

We will praise you with the sun and the moon,
with the sea and all that it holds.
Earth and heaven sing the glory of God,
all creation praises your name.

O my soul, bless the Lord;
all that lives, bless the Lord.
Praise your name above all names;
all that breathes, bless the Lord.

You trees that grow, the winter snow,
you works of God, bless the Lord.
The winds that howl, the thunder's growl,
sing the power of your name.

▶ When has the kindness, love, or other virtues of persons around you called you to praise or prayer?

Prayer

O Lord,
when I look at your heavens, the work of your fingers,
    the moon and the stars that you have established;
what are human beings that you are mindful of them,
    mortals that you care for them?

Pause to recall the gifts God has given you personally.

Yet you have made them a little lower than God,
    and crowned them with glory and honor.
You have given them dominion over the works of your hands;
    you have put all things under their feet,
    all sheep and oxen, and also the beasts of the field,
    the birds of the air, and the fish of the sea,
    whatever passes along the paths of the seas.
O Lord, our Sovereign, how majestic is your name in all the earth!

(Ps 8:3–9)

Actions

• A steward is one who cares for the possessions of another. Resolve to be a good steward of at least one of the gifts of creation, for example, water.

• Help provide others with clean water, air, or some other resource, either through writing to the appropriate agency or making a donation to a charitable organization.

Close

End your prayer by listening quietly once again to the song "We Will Praise You."

Turning Back to God

"Lord, this time change our hearts."

Quiet your mind and heart and center on God's presence. Let your whole being enter into prayer.

Invitation to Pray

We have a merciful and loving God! Praise and thank God and begin in the name of the Father, and of the Son, and of the Holy Spirit. Amen.

Prepare Your Heart

Sin is a reality in today's world and in the life of each Christian. Pause here for just a moment to reflect on how you see sin affecting the world. How do you see it in your life?

If you are with others, share your reflections if you wish. If alone, reflect in silence.

The Word of God

They heard the sound of the Lord God walking in the garden at the time of the evening breeze, and the man and his wife hid themselves from the presence of the Lord God among the trees of the garden. But the Lord God called to the man, and said to him, "Where are you?" He said, "I heard the sound of you in the garden, and I was afraid, because I was naked; and I hid myself." He said, "Who told you that you were naked? Have you eaten from the tree of which I commanded you not to eat?" (Gen 3:8–11)

Reflection

If you are with others, share your reflections if you wish. If alone, reflect in silence, then write notes in the space provided.

▶ What are the thoughts, desires, feelings, memories, or fears within your own heart that need to be changed by God's grace?

▶ What things most tempt you away from the teachings of the gospel?

▶ How have you experienced God's mercy when you failed in the past?

Meditation on Music

Allow a moment or two for prayerful silence, then listen to or sing along with "Change Our Hearts" by Rory Cooney (track 9 on CD).

Change our hearts this time, your word says it can be.
Change our minds this time, your life could make us free.
We are the people your call set apart,
Lord, this time change our hearts.

Brought by your hand to the edge of our dreams,
one foot in paradise, one in the waste;
drawn by your promises, still we are lured
by the shadows and the chains we leave behind.

Now as we watch you stretch out your hands,
offering abundances, fullness of joy.
Your milk and honey seem distant, unreal,
when we have bread and water in our hands.

Prayer

O God of goodness and light,
　　we come to you in prayer.
Accept what is within our hearts
　　and hold us close to you.

Brief sacred pause

When we are tempted to be less,
　　less than you created us to be,
　　less than you have taught us to be,
　　O God, bring us home to you!

Pause to recall those times when you most need Christ's light. Name those people in your life or in the world who need it now.

Christ, Son of the living God,
　　who had mercy on sinners,
　　we need your forgiveness now.
We pray for the strength to forgive others
　　and to ask for forgiveness. Amen.

Actions

• Make a firm resolution to forgive someone against whom you are holding a grudge.

• Commit yourself to celebrating the sacrament of reconciliation.

Close

End your prayer by listening quietly once again to the song "Change Our Hearts."

Jesus Is the Messiah!

"You have made us in your image."

Quiet your mind and heart and center on God's presence. Let your whole being enter into prayer.

Invitation to Pray

Christ is our light and our life! Turn your heart now to God, and begin in the name of the Father, and of the Son, and of the Holy Spirit. Amen.

Prepare Your Heart

In Christ, we see God's amazing love for us. How did Christ express that love?

If you are with others, share your reflections if you wish. If alone, reflect in silence.

The Word of God

Let the same mind be in you that was in Christ Jesus,
    who, though he was in the form of God,
      did not regard equality with God as something to be exploited,
      but emptied himself, taking the form of a slave,
      being born in human likeness.
And being found in human form,
    he humbled himself

and became obedient to the point of death—
even death on a cross.

Therefore God also highly exalted him
and gave him the name that is above every name,
so that at the name of Jesus every knee should bend,
in heaven and on earth and under the earth,
and every tongue should confess that Jesus Christ is Lord,
to the glory of God the Father. (Phil 2:5–11)

REFLECTION

If you are with others, share your reflections if you wish. If alone, reflect in silence, then write notes in the space provided.

▶ How do your words, thoughts, actions, and desires reflect Christ?

▶ What steps do you take to know Christ better through Scripture, to love Christ more by celebrating the sacraments?

MEDITATION ON MUSIC

Allow a moment or two for prayerful silence, then listen to or sing along with "God, Beyond All Names" by Bernadette Farrell (track 8 on CD).

God, beyond all names, you have made us in your image;
we are like you, we reflect you; we are woman, we are man.

All around us we have known you, all creation lives to hold you.
In our living and our dying we are bringing you to birth.

God, beyond all words, all creation tells your story;
you have shaken with our laughter, you have trembled with our tears.

Prayer

Christ, Son of God, our Savior,
> you are the good shepherd,
> the living vine, the living water.
You care for us and quench our thirst,
> hear the prayers of our hearts.

Brief sacred pause

Be our way through the difficulties of life.
Be our truth so we may always judge rightly.
Be our life, now and in eternity.

Pause to recall the moments when you felt closest to Christ.

May your resurrection be our hope.
May your teachings be our light.
May we share your love with our sisters and brothers. Amen.

Actions

• Choose one of the Beatitudes and let it guide your decisions.

• Share Jesus' love by doing an act of kindness for someone.

Close

End your prayer by listening quietly once again to the song "God, Beyond All Names."

Mary, God's Mother and Ours

"Morning star, so strong and bright."

Quiet your mind and heart and center on God's presence. Let your whole being enter into prayer.

Invitation to Pray

We bless our God for the wonders of his love! Turn your hearts to God with love and begin in the name of the Father, and of the Son, and of the Holy Spirit. Amen.

Prepare Your Heart

Mary's word *Adsum* in Latin means "Here I am"—yes, I come to do your will. How do you respond when you sense God is calling you?

If you are with others, share your reflections if you wish. If alone, reflect in silence.

The Word of God

In those days Mary set out and went with haste to a Judean town in the hill country, where she entered the house of Zechariah and greeted Elizabeth. When Elizabeth heard Mary's greeting, the child leapt in her womb. And Elizabeth was filled with the Holy Spirit and exclaimed with a loud cry, "Blessed are you among women, and blessed is the fruit of your womb. And why has this happened to me, that the mother of my Lord comes to me? For as soon as I heard the sound of your greeting, the child in my womb leapt for joy. And blessed is she who believed that there would be a fulfillment of what was spoken to her by the Lord." (Lk 1:39–45)

REFLECTION

If you are with others, share your reflections if you wish. If alone, reflect in silence, then write notes in the space provided.

▶ What place does Mary have in your life?

▶ How does Mary's example lead you closer to her Son Jesus Christ?

MEDITATION ON MUSIC

Allow a moment or two for prayerful silence, then listen to or sing along with "Hail Mary, Gentle Woman" by Carey Landry (track 10 on CD).

Hail Mary, full of grace, the Lord is with you.
Blessed are you among women and blest is the fruit
of your womb, Jesus.
Holy Mary, Mother of God, pray for us sinners now
and at the hour of death. Amen.

Gentle woman, quiet light, morning star, so strong and bright,
gentle Mother, peaceful dove, teach us wisdom; teach us love.

You were chosen by the Father;
you were chosen for the Son.
You were chosen from all women
and for woman, shining one.

Prayer

Loving God, we thank you
    for having chosen Mary
    to be the mother of your Son.
May she be for us a model
    of faith and love.

Brief sacred pause

My soul magnifies the Lord,
    and my spirit rejoices in God my Savior,
    for he has looked with favor on
    the lowliness of his servant.
Surely, from now on all generations will call me blessed,
    for the Mighty One has done great things for me,
    and holy is his name.
His mercy is for those who fear him
    from generation to generation.
He has shown strength with his arm;
    he has scattered the proud in the thoughts of their hearts.
He has brought down the powerful from their thrones,
    and lifted up the lowly;
he has filled the hungry with good things,
    and sent the rich away empty.
He has helped his servant Israel,
    in remembrance of his mercy,
    according to the promise he made to our ancestors,
    to Abraham and to his descendants forever.

Actions

• Imitate Mary's faith when facing a difficult choice or situation.

• Entrust to Mary's prayers someone who is in need.

Close

End your prayer by listening quietly once again to the song "Hail Mary, Gentle Woman."

Christ Taught about the Kingdom

"Be the light of Christ in the world."

Quiet your mind and heart and center on God's presence. Let your whole being enter into prayer.

Invitation to Pray

Our God is a God of mystery! Turn your hearts to him in wonder and praise, and begin in the name of the Father, and of the Son, and of the Holy Spirit. Amen.

Prepare Your Heart

By the waters of John's baptism, Jesus began his ministry. What connection do the waters of baptism have to your ministry? How has this affected your attitude to your ministry?

If you are with others, share your reflections if you wish. If alone, reflect in silence.

The Word of God

Then he took a loaf of bread, and when he had given thanks, he broke it and gave it to them, saying, "This is my body, which is given for you. Do this in remembrance of me." And he did the same with the cup after supper, saying, "This cup that is poured out for you is the new covenant in my blood." (Lk 22:19–20)

Reflection

If you are with others, share your reflections if you wish. If alone, reflect in silence, then write notes in the space provided.

▶ Recall the ways in which Christ has healed you in your life.

▶ In what concrete ways do you bring Christ's light to others?

▶ What connection do you find between the Sunday assembly gathered to celebrate the Eucharist and the kingdom of heaven?

Meditation on Music

Allow a moment or two for prayerful silence, then listen to or sing along with "Light of Christ" by Tom Kendzia (track 11 on CD).

Be the light of Christ in the world.
Bring the nations God's own love.
Set a blaze in the night, make the earth shine bright.
Be the light of Christ to the world.

No more tears, no more pain,
no more hunger; we'll laugh again.
God of glory will guide our ways.
God of mercy will light our days.

As the stars that shine in the heavens,
so our light will shine on earth.
Risen Jesus has conquered the night
and freed us from death with this light.

Prayer

Christ, you have taught us
    about the kingdom of heaven.
You formed a community of men and women,
    a community that continues in the Church.
This Church is a pathway to your kingdom.

Brief sacred pause

We pray now
    for the body of Christ that it may grow and be strong;
    for the poor, that your kingdom
        may be proclaimed to them;
    for unity and mercy to replace division;
    for the strength to serve as Christ taught;
    for all who are weak or lost
        that they may be brought back into the fold.

Pause to recall what Jesus taught about the kingdom, and to reflect on how you have lived that teaching.

Jesus, may our hearts always be open
    to the poor and needy.
May we die with you
    in order to live fully.
May we strive for conversion of heart
    and help lead others along that path. Amen.

Actions

• Make your family meal time a time of sharing.

• Take a positive step to serve the needy or neglected persons in your area.

Close

End your prayer by listening quietly once again to the song "Light of Christ."

Jesus Died that We Might Live

"Love one another, as I have loved you."

Quiet your mind and heart and center on God's presence. Let your whole being enter into prayer.

Invitation to Pray

Our God is love and life! Turn your hearts now to God, and begin in the name of the Father, and of the Son, and of the Holy Spirit. Amen.

Prepare Your Heart

How is the cross a sign of God's love?

If you are with others, share your reflections if you wish. If alone, reflect in silence.

The Word of God

Beloved, let us love one another, because love is from God; everyone who loves is born of God and knows God. Whoever does not love does not know God, for God is love. God's love was revealed among us in this way: God sent his only Son into the world so that we might live through him. In this is love, not that we loved God but that he loved us and sent his Son to be the atoning sacrifice for our sins. Beloved, since God loved us so much, we also ought to love one another. No one has ever seen God; if we love one another, God lives in us, and his love is perfected in us. (1 Jn 4:7–12)

REFLECTION

If you are with others, share your reflections if you wish. If alone, reflect in silence, then write notes in the space provided.

▶ How is your life filled with love? In what ways do you need to cultivate a loving heart?

▶ Remember a time someone reached out to you in love when you did not expect it. How was this a sign for you of God's love?

MEDITATION ON MUSIC

Allow a moment or two for prayerful silence, then listen to or sing along with "Love One Another" by Bob Dufford, SJ (track 12 on CD).

Love one another as I have loved you.
Care for each other. I have cared for you.
Bear each other's burdens. Bind each other's wounds;
and so you will know my return.

My friends, do you know what I have done for you?
I have washed your feet with my hands.
If I, your Lord, have knelt at your feet,
you should do at each other's feet as I have done for you.

When the world will hate you and revile you,
when they laugh at your care for the poor,
when they hold you in darkness and imprison your tongues,
remember how they listened to me.

Text based on Jn 14-16; 1 Cor 13. Music and text © 1987, Robert J. Dufford, SJ. Published by OCP Publications. All rights reserved.

Prayer

O loving God, you sent your only Son, Jesus Christ,
    to bear the wounds of our sin,
    to save us and to heal us.
Accept our prayers in the name of your Son.

Pause and reflect on Jesus' sacrifice.

Soul of Christ,
    sanctify us.
Body of Christ,
    save us.
Blood flowing from the side of Christ,
    wash away our sins.

Pause and recall all the persons in the world in need of redemption and healing.

In love, Lord, we pray
    for all who suffer,
    for those who care for the sick and dying,
    for those who are lonely or abandoned.
May we have the goodness to serve those in need
    of comfort and care.
O God, keep us now and always. Amen.

Actions

• Read the passion and death of Christ, either alone or with your family.

• Plan to participate, as much as is possible, in the Triduum celebrated at your parish.

Close

End your prayer by listening quietly once again to the song "Love One Another."

Encounter the Risen Christ

"And he will raise you up on eagle's wings."

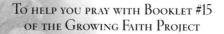

Quiet your mind and heart and center on God's presence. Let your whole being enter into prayer.

Invitation to Pray

Jesus is our Risen Lord! Sing alleluia as you begin in the name of the Father, and of the Son, and of the Holy Spirit. Amen.

Prepare Your Heart

When we speak of resurrection, we mean transformation to a new and glorious life. What daily dyings and risings have you experienced in your life? How does Christ transform you?

If you are with others, share your reflections if you wish. If alone, reflect in silence.

The Word of God

And very early on the first day of the week, when the sun had risen, the women went to the tomb. They had been saying to one another, "Who will roll away the stone for us from the entrance to the tomb?" When they looked up, they saw that the stone, which was very large, had already been rolled back. As they entered the tomb, they saw a young man, dressed in a white robe, sitting on the right side; and they were alarmed. But he said to them, "Do not be alarmed; you are looking for Jesus of Nazareth, who was crucified. He has been raised; he is not here. Look, there is the place they laid him. But go, tell his disciples and Peter that he is going ahead of you to Galilee; there you will see him, just as he told you." (Mk 16:2–7)

Reflection

If you are with others, share your reflections if you wish. If alone, reflect in silence, then write notes in the space provided.

▶ Which is your favorite gospel "resurrection story"? Why is it your favorite and what does it say to you?

▶ In what ways do you experience the presence of the risen Christ in your life? How does this presence transform you?

Meditation on Music

Allow a moment or two for prayerful silence, then listen to or sing along with "On Eagle's Wings" by Michael Joncas (track 13 on CD).

You who dwell in the shelter of the Lord,
who abide in his shadow for life,
say to the Lord: "My refuge, my rock in whom I trust!"

And he will raise you up on eagle's wings,
bear you on the breath of dawn,
make you to shine like the sun,
and hold you in the palm of his hand.

You need not fear the terror of the night,
nor the arrow that flies by day;
though thousands fall about you,
near you it shall not come.

Prayer

O God of mystery,
  rejoicing in the power of the resurrection,
  we ask that we all may rise with Christ your Son.

Pause and reflect on the event of Jesus' resurrection.

Lord Jesus, you are our resurrection
  and our life.
You have cast away the shadows of sin and death.
May our journey of conversion
  lead us to new life in you.

Pause to remember all those who need the healing power of Christ's resurrection.

We pray now for persons who need
  to experience the resurrection in their own lives:
  for those who are grieving,
  for those who are dying,
  for those who are suffering from addiction,
  for all of us who seek to grow closer to you,
    O risen Lord.
May you be our life and our hope. Amen.

Actions

• Do something meaningful to celebrate Jesus' resurrection. Spend a special day with the family; recall your own baptism with a short prayer service before your evening meal; or treat yourself to a real day of rest.

• Bring the joy of the resurrection to someone during the week through an act of kindness or service.

Close

End your prayer by listening quietly once again to the song "On Eagle's Wings."

The Holy Spirit Enflames Hearts

"My soul is thirsting for you, O Lord."

Quiet your mind and heart and center on God's presence. Let your whole being enter into prayer.

Invitation to Pray

The Spirit of God is love! Open your hearts to his love, and begin in the name of the Father, and of the Son, and of the Holy Spirit. Amen.

Prepare Your Heart

The Spirit of God blows wherever it will, and fills our hearts with gifts of grace. Pause a moment to reflect. How do you experience the Spirit's presence in your life?

If you are with others, share your reflections if you wish. If alone, reflect in silence.

The Word of God

When the day of Pentecost had come, they were all together in one place. And suddenly from heaven there came a sound like the rush of a violent wind, and it filled the entire house where they were sitting. Divided tongues, as of fire, appeared among them, and a tongue rested on each of them. All of them were filled with the

Holy Spirit and began to speak in other languages, as the Spirit gave them ability. (Acts 2:1–4)

REFLECTION

If you are with others, share your reflections if you wish. If alone, reflect in silence, then write notes in the space provided.

▶ How does the Holy Spirit's presence shape your life?

▶ How do you experience the Spirit's presence in the Church?

MEDITATION ON MUSIC

Allow a moment or two for prayerful silence, then listen to or sing along with "My Soul Is Thirsting" by Steve Angrisano (track 14 on CD).

My soul is thirsting for you, O Lord,
thirsting for you, my God.
My soul is thirsting for you, O Lord,
thirsting for you, my God.
Thirsting for you, my God,
thirsting for you, my God.

O God, you are my God, and I will always praise you.
In the shadow of your wings I cling to you
and you hold me high.

I will never be afraid, for I will not be abandoned.
Even when the road grows long and weary
your love will rescue me.

Prayer

Relying on the presence of the Spirit of God with us,
    we pray together:

Abide, O Spirit of life!
Let peace fill our hearts,
Let love fill our minds.
Make us loving disciples of Christ.
May we all be one,
May we all be yours,
    abide, O Spirit of Life!

Pause and ask to be open to the gifts of the Spirit.

We ask you to guide all our actions,
    show the path we should walk.
We desire to know what will please you.
Abide, O Spirit of Life!

May we walk together in justice.
Teach us wisdom, unite all our hearts.
May your grace be here now to guide us.
Abide, O Spirit of Life!
May God bless us and keep us, now and always. Amen.

Actions

• For centuries, we have blessed one another by laying hands on each other. Bless someone today in need of the Spirit's light and grace.

• Let the gifts of the Holy Spirit make you more sensitive to and aware of the Spirit's action within you, and more open to the practice of the virtues, especially one you feel you need most.

Close

End your prayer by listening quietly once again to the song "My Soul Is Thirsting."

The Mystery of the Church

"Draw us forth to the table of life."

Quiet your mind and heart and center on God's presence. Let your whole being enter into prayer.

Invitation to Pray

Our God is the God of love and unity! Turn your hearts now to God and begin in the name of the Father, and of the Son, and of the Holy Spirit. Amen.

Prepare Your Heart

Have you thought of yourself as a temple of the Holy Spirit? Apart from theological reflections, what feelings does this image evoke in you?

If you are with others, share your reflections if you wish. If alone, reflect in silence.

The Word of God

For though I am absent in body, yet I am with you in spirit, and I rejoice to see your morale and the firmness of your faith in Christ. As you therefore have received Christ Jesus the Lord, continue to live your lives in him, rooted and built up in him and established in the faith, just as you were taught, abounding in thanksgiving. (Col 2:5–6)

REFLECTION

If you are with others, share your reflections if you wish. If alone, reflect in silence, then write notes in the space provided.

▶ In what ways does your relationship with others give you glimpses of Christ's love?

▶ How does your gathering with others for prayer change your life?

MEDITATION ON MUSIC

Allow a moment or two for prayerful silence, then listen to or sing along with "Gather Your People" by Bob Hurd (track 3 on CD).

Gather your people, O Lord. Gather your people, O Lord.
One bread, one body, one spirit of love.
Gather your people, O Lord.

Draw us forth to the table of life:
brothers and sisters, each of us called to walk in your light.

We are parts of the body of Christ,
needing each other, each of the gifts the Spirit provides.

PRAYER

Loving God, knowing that you are with us
    when we gather, we ask you to nourish
        the body of Christ, to become the body of Christ.
Hear the prayer we offer you with grateful hearts.

Brief sacred pause

Lord, we pray for your Church,
　　the bride of Christ and the temple of the Holy Spirit.
When we gather as Church, may we praise your name
　　and recall our membership as people of God
　　through faith and baptism.

Pause and reflect on the Church's mission to be the sacrament of salvation.

O God of all goodness,
　　may we fulfill our mission as members of your Church,
　　whether we are called to be apostles,
　　teachers, prophets...whatever it may be.
Teach us to always keep in mind the good
　　of your people
　　and be selfless in our service. Amen.

ACTIONS

• Resolve to show God's care for someone who lives alone.

• Commit yourself to full and active participation in the Sunday liturgy.

CLOSE

End your prayer by listening quietly once again to the song "Gather Your People."

Characteristics of the Church

"Bring the nations God's own love."

Quiet your mind and heart and center on God's presence. Let your whole being enter into prayer.

Invitation to Pray

We praise Christ who calls us to live in love! Turn your heart now to God, and begin in the name of the Father, and of the Son, and of the Holy Spirit. Amen.

Prepare Your Hearts

"The gifts he gave were…to equip the saints for the world of ministry, for building up the body of Christ, until all of us come to the unity of the faith" (Eph 4:11–13). What gifts have you been given for ministry and for building up the body of Christ?

If you are with others, share your reflections if you wish. If alone, reflect in silence.

The Word of God

The gifts he gave were that some would be apostles, some prophets, some evangelists, some pastors and teachers, to equip the saints for the work of ministry, for building up the body of Christ, until all of us come to the unity of the faith and of the knowledge of the Son of God, to maturity, to the measure of the full stature of Christ. We must no longer be children, tossed to and fro and blown about by every wind of doctrine, by people's trickery, by their craftiness in deceitful scheming. But speaking the truth in love, we must grow up in every way into him who is the head, into Christ, from whom the whole body, joined and knit together by every ligament with which it is equipped, as each part is working properly, promotes the body's growth in building itself up in love. (Eph 4:11–16)

REFLECTION

If you are with others, share your reflections if you wish. If alone, reflect in silence, then write notes in the space provided.

▶ How do you gain strength from others to live as a Christian?

▶ How do you support others on their journey of faith?

MEDITATION ON MUSIC

Allow a moment or two for prayerful silence, then listen to or sing along with "Light of Christ" by Tom Kendzia (track 11 on CD).

Be the light of Christ in the world.
Bring the nations God's own love.
Set a blaze in the night, make the earth shine bright.
Be the light of Christ to the world.

No more tears, no more pain, no more hunger; we'll laugh again.
God of glory will guide our ways.
God of mercy will light our days.

As the stars that shine in the heavens,
so our light will shine on earth.
Risen Jesus has conquered the night
and freed us from death with this light.

Prayer

O God, trusting in your goodness and generosity,
> we ask you to accept the prayers we carry in our hearts.

Brief sacred pause

Lord Jesus, we pray for all those
> who do not yet know your gospel.

May they seek God's will with a sincere heart.
Moved by your grace, may they try to do God's will
> as they know it through their conscience.

Pause and recall the holiness to which Christ calls the members of the Church.

O Jesus, good shepherd,
> lead us all to conversion of mind and heart,
> to conversion of life,
> so that your Church may shine as an example to all people
> > of the way to God.

We ask this in your name. Amen.

Actions

• Build up unity in your own family or neighborhood by some action, however small.

• Resolve to change one habit in your life that hinders your growth in Christ.

Close

End your prayer by listening quietly once again to the song "Light of Christ."

We Are the Church

"I will hold your people in my heart."

Quiet your mind and heart and center on God's presence. Let your whole being enter into prayer.

Invitation to Pray

Our God gathers us as one. Thanks be to God for all God's gifts! Let your whole being praise God, and begin in the name of the Father, and of the Son, and of the Holy Spirit. Amen.

Prepare Your Heart

Our pastors stand among us as servants. When have you experienced their servant-leadership? What does service call you to be or to do?

If you are with others, share your reflections if you wish. If alone, reflect in silence.

The Word of God

But you are a chosen race, a royal priesthood, a holy nation, God's own people, in order that you may proclaim the mighty acts of him who called you out of darkness into his marvelous light.
Once you were not a people,
  but now you are God's people;
  once you had not received mercy,
  but now you have received mercy.

(Pt 2:9–10)

Reflection

If you are with others, share your reflections if you wish. If alone, reflect in silence, then write notes in the space provided.

▶ When in your life have you done something because you felt called to do so?

▶ Have you ever maintained a stony heart, refusing to listen to the promptings of the Holy Spirit?

Meditation on Music

Allow a moment or two for prayerful silence, then listen to or sing along with "Here I Am, Lord" by Dan Schutte (track 15 on CD).

I, the Lord of sea and sky, I have heard my people cry.
All who dwell in dark and sin my hand will save.
I, who made the stars of night, I will make their darkness bright.
Who will bear my light to them? Whom shall I send?

Here I am, Lord.
Is it I, Lord?
I have heard you calling in the night.
I will go, Lord, if you lead me.
I will hold your people in my heart.

I, the Lord of snow and rain, I have borne my people's pain.
I have wept for love of them. They turn away.
I will break their hearts of stone, give them hearts for love alone.
I will speak my word to them. Whom shall I send?

Text: Based on Isaiah 6. Text and music © 1981, OCP Publications. All rights reserved.

Prayer

Loving God, as your people
  we are ready to respond to your call to serve.
May we share in Christ's own mission
  to care for the poor and proclaim the gospel to all.

Brief sacred pause

Lord Jesus, we pray for the poor of the world
  and for those who offer them help.
We pray for all who work for a more just society.
We pray for the oppressed
  and those whom society counts for nothing.
May we invite them to experience the love of God.

Pause and thank God for his goodness.

My soul magnifies the Lord,
  and my spirit rejoices in God my Savior.
His mercy is for those who fear him
  from generation to generation.
He has shown strength with his arm;
  he has scattered the proud
  in the thoughts of their hearts.
He has filled the hungry with good things,
  and sent the rich away empty.
Praise to you, Lord. Amen.

Action

• Resolve to assist your parish community in some undertaking, such as spending time at a soup kitchen.

• Reach out to someone who no longer participates at Mass.

Close

End your prayer by listening quietly once again to the song "Here I Am, Lord."

The Communion of Saints

"Follow me, follow me."

Quiet your mind and heart and center on God's presence. Let your whole being enter into prayer.

INVITATION TO PRAY

Our God's love is everlasting! Let your whole being turn to God as you begin in the name of the Father, and of the Son, and of the Holy Spirit. Amen.

PREPARE YOUR HEART

The purpose of human life is made clear by Christ. How do you describe that purpose for yourself?

If you are with others, share your reflections if you wish. If alone, reflect in silence.

THE WORD OF GOD

Then Jesus told his disciples, "If any want to become my followers, let them deny themselves and take up their cross and follow me. For those who want to save their life will lose it, and those who lose their life for my sake will find it. For what will it profit them if they gain the whole world but forfeit their life? Or what will they give in return for their life? (Mt 16:24–26)

Reflection

If you are with others, share your reflections if you wish. If alone, reflect in silence, then write notes in the space provided.

▶ How does Jesus' life strengthen you to take up your cross?

▶ In what ways have you given your life for the sake of Christ?

Meditation on Music

Allow a moment or two for prayerful silence, then listen to or sing along with "I, the Lord" by Tom Kendzia (track 16 on CD).

I, the Lord, am with you,
always by your side.
Come and take my hand,
for I will lead you home.
Follow me, follow me.

I am the resurrection,
and I am the life;
if you believe in me,
you shall live forever.

You shall have new life
and live it to the full.
Turn your sorrow into joy,
for life has just begun.

Prayer

Loving God, filled with the presence of the Spirit,
    we pray for the strength and light
    to follow in Christ's footsteps.
Please hear our prayers and bless all who strive for holiness.

Pause and reflect on Jesus' call to take up our crosses.

Lord Jesus, give us the strength to follow you
    in the face of trial.
May we be faithful to our commitment to you
    and be salt and light for our wounded world.

Pause and recall Jesus' love for others, a love imitated by the saints.

Lord, like the saints who down through history
    walked in your way, the way of the gospel,
    may we show compassion for those who need healing,
    pray for those whose faith wavers,
    and lead to you all who wait to meet you.
We ask all this in your name. Amen.

Actions

• Pray to and imitate the saint whom you feel closest to.

• Offer the good works of your day for someone who is faltering in their belief in Christ.

Close

End your prayer by listening quietly once again to the song "I, the Lord."

Liturgy: Source of Our Lives

"How can your soul find rest, except for the Lord?"

Quiet your mind and heart and center on God's presence. Let your whole being enter into prayer.

INVITATION TO PRAY

The Spirit guides our prayer! Thank God for the Spirit's gifts, and begin in the name of the Father, and of the Son, and of the Holy Spirit. Amen.

PREPARE YOUR HEART

The sacraments help us live our Christian life. How do they help you?

If you are with others, share your reflections if you wish. If alone, reflect in silence.

THE WORD OF GOD

I give you thanks, O Lord, with my whole heart;
    before the gods I sing your praise;
I bow down toward your holy temple
    and give thanks to your name for your steadfast love
    and your faithfulness;
    for you have exalted your name
    and your word above everything.

All the kings of the earth shall praise you, O Lord,
   for they have heard the words of your mouth.
They shall sing of the ways of the Lord,
   for great is the glory of the Lord.
For though the Lord is high, he regards the lowly;
   but the haughty he perceives from far away.
Your steadfast love, O Lord, endures forever.
Do not forsake the work of your hands.

(Ps 138:1–2, 4–6, 8b)

REFLECTION

If you are with others, share your reflections if you wish. If alone, reflect in silence, then write notes in the space provided.

▶ In what part of the liturgy do you most experience God's presence?

▶ How fully do you participate in the Sunday liturgy?

MEDITATION ON MUSIC

Allow a moment or two for prayerful silence, then listen to or sing along with "Come to the Water" by John Foley, SJ (track 1 on CD).

O let all who thirst, let them come to the water.
And let all who have nothing, let them come to the Lord:
without money, without price.
Why should you pay the price, except for the Lord?

And let all who toil, let them come to the water.
And let all who are weary, let them come to the Lord:
all who labor, without rest.
How can your soul find rest, except for the Lord?

Text: Based on Isaiah 55:1-2; Matthew 11:28-30. Text and music © 1978, John B. Foley, SJ and OCP Publications. All rights reserved.

Prayer

O loving God, you are the source of all the gifts of creation.
  Hear our prayer and bless all who seek you in their hearts.

Brief sacred pause

Merciful God, you have blessed us in Christ,
  so that we might be your adopted sons
  and daughters in the Spirit.
We praise and thank you for
  the presence of Christ in the liturgy.
Through the celebration of these rites,
  you nourish us with the grace of your sacraments.

Pause and reflect on the action of the Holy Spirit in the Church.

O Holy Spirit, through Christ's body, the Church,
  you dispense the mystery of salvation.
Through the actions of the Church in the liturgy,
  we participate in the heavenly liturgy.
Help us prepare to encounter Christ in the sacraments
  and to bring the living waters of his word and his life to others.
We ask this in Christ's name. Amen.

Actions

• Resolve to receive the Eucharist with more awareness and love.

• Commit yourself to looking for the "holy" during your day.

Close

End your prayer by listening quietly once again to the song "Come to the Water."

Celebrating the Liturgy

"Come to the table of plenty!"

Quiet your mind and heart and center on God's presence. Let your whole being enter into prayer.

INVITATION TO PRAY

Our God is the God of our salvation! Praise God with grateful hearts and begin in the name of the Father, and of the Son, and of the Holy Spirit. Amen.

PREPARE YOUR HEART

Music helps us lift our hearts in prayer. What sort of music does this best for you? Has a particular song been an important part of your journey of faith? What and why?

If you are with others, share your reflections if you wish. If alone, reflect in silence.

THE WORD OF GOD

Let the word of Christ dwell in you richly; teach and admonish one another in all wisdom; and with gratitude in your hearts sing psalms, hymns, and spiritual songs to God. And whatever you do, in word or deed, do everything in the name of the Lord Jesus, giving thanks to God the Father through him. (Col 3:16–17)

REFLECTION

If you are with others, share your reflections if you wish. If alone, reflect in silence, then write notes in the space provided.

▶ How is the Mass a celebration of present and future promise?

▶ What in your daily life has changed as a result of an experience in liturgical prayer?

MEDITATION ON MUSIC

Allow a moment or two for prayerful silence, then listen to or sing along with "Table of Plenty" by Dan Schutte (track 17 on CD).

Come to the feast of heaven and earth!
Come to the table of plenty!
God will provide for all that we need,
here at the table of plenty.

O come and sit at my table
where saints and sinners are friends.
I wait to welcome the lost and lonely
to share the cup of my love.

My bread will ever sustain you
 through days of sorrow and woe.
My wine will flow like a sea of gladness
to flood the depths of your soul.

Prayer

Loving God, we welcome your love and light
    into our hearts each day.
Accept our prayers in union with the prayer of the Church.

Pause and reflect on the meaning of the symbols used in the liturgy.

Lord God, the symbols and gestures we use in the liturgy
    speak to us of your love
    and the life you fill us with in abundance.
We use them to express our faith.
Strengthen our faith in you and our love for you
    and for our sisters and brothers.

Pause and recall how we use signs and symbols in our daily lives.

O Lord Jesus, you used so many signs in your ministry
    to show your love and care for others:
    washing, anointing, breaking bread.
May we use these same signs to serve others in your name:
    all those who are hungry,
    all who thirst for you,
    the homeless and abandoned,
    all who feel far from God.
Please guide and bless our efforts. Amen.

Actions

• Reflect on an image that connects you most closely to God and let it lead you into prayer.

• Take time to celebrate life, even in a small way.

Close

End your prayer by listening quietly once again to the song "Table of Plenty."

Baptism: Birth into New Life

"I will hold your people in my heart."

Quiet your mind and heart and center on God's presence. Let your whole being enter into prayer.

Invitation to Pray

God gives us new life in water and the Spirit. Thanks be to God! Let your whole being enter into prayer and begin in the name of the Father, and of the Son, and of the Holy Spirit. Amen.

Prepare Your Heart

In baptism we receive the Holy Spirit and are initiated into life in the Church. What are your baptismal promises? What do those promises call you to be or to do as a Christian?

If you are with others, share your reflections if you wish. If alone, reflect in silence.

The Word of God

Now when they heard this, they were cut to the heart and said to Peter and to the other apostles, "Brothers, what should we do?" Peter said to them, "Repent, and be baptized every one of you in the name of Jesus Christ so that your sins may be forgiven; and you will receive the gift of the Holy Spirit. For the promise is for you, for your children, and for all who are far away, everyone whom the Lord our God calls to him." (Acts 2:37–39)

REFLECTION

If you are with others, share your reflections if you wish. If alone, reflect in silence, then write notes in the space provided.

▶ How is your baptism the beginning of a relationship? With whom? For what purpose?

▶ What comes to mind when you enter church and dip your hand into the font (baptismal font or font of holy water)?

MEDITATION ON MUSIC

Allow a moment or two for prayerful silence, then listen to or sing along with "Here I Am, Lord" by Dan Schutte (track 15 on CD).

I, the Lord of sea and sky, I have heard my people cry.
All who dwell in dark and sin my hand will save.
I, who made the stars of night, I will make their darkness bright.
Who will bear my light to them? Whom shall I send?

Here I am, Lord. Is it I, Lord?
I have heard you calling in the night.
I will go, Lord, if you lead me.
I will hold your people in my heart.

I, the Lord of snow and rain, I have borne my people's pain.
I have wept for love of them. They turn away.
I will break their hearts of stone, give them hearts for love alone.
I will speak my word to them. Whom shall I send?

Prayer

Loving God, as baptized believers,
    we offer our prayers of thanksgiving to you,
    confident that you will accept them in love.

Pause and reflect on the tremendous gift of baptism.

God of grace and beginnings,
    you washed us in the waters of rebirth
    and called us your sons and daughters.
May we daily enter more fully
    into the life and death of Christ,
to love more deeply and generously
    as we walk in his footsteps.

Pause to recall your baptismal promises.

Lord Jesus, when we were baptized
    and initiated into your body, the Church,
we promised to reject Satan and sin,
    so as to live in the freedom of God's children.
We made our profession of faith.
Give us the strength and light
    to daily keep those promises
    and live up to that faith.
We ask this in your name. Amen.

Actions

• Resolve that when you make the sign of the cross, you will recall your baptism and baptismal promises.

• Pray for all those who do not yet know Christ.

Close

End your prayer by listening quietly once again to the song "Here I Am, Lord."

Confirmation: Gift of the Spirit

"Your Spirit, O God, is upon me."

Quiet your mind and heart and center on God's presence. Let your whole being enter into prayer.

Invitation to Pray

The Spirit of our God fills us with blessings. Thanks be to God! Turn your hearts to God and begin in the name of the Father, and of the Son, and of the Holy Spirit. Amen.

Prepare Your Heart

The Spirit brings firmness of purpose to us. How do you experience the Spirit bringing such strength? How do the gifts of the Spirit play a part in your daily life?

If you are with others, share your reflections if you wish. If alone, reflect in silence.

The Word of God

If you love me, you will keep my commandments. And I will ask the Father, and he will give you another Advocate, to be with you for ever. This is the Spirit of truth, whom the world cannot receive, because it neither sees him nor knows him. You know him, because he abides with you, and he will be in you. (Jn 14:15–17)

Reflection

If you are with others, share your reflections if you wish. If alone, reflect in silence, then write notes in the space provided.

▶ What does it mean to you that you have been anointed?

▶ What does being an anointed one of God call you to be or to do?

Meditation on Music

Allow a moment or two for prayerful silence, then listen to or sing along with "You Have Anointed Me" by Mike Balhoff, Gary Daigle, and Darryl Ducote (track 18 on CD).

To bring glad tidings to the lowly, to heal the broken heart,
you have anointed me.
To proclaim liberty to captives, release to prisoners,
you have anointed me.

Your Spirit, O God, is upon me,
you have anointed me.

To announce a year of favor, to comfort those who mourn,
you have anointed me.
To give them the oil of gladness, and share a mantle of joy,
you have anointed me.

© 1981 by Damean Music. Used with permission.

Prayer

Loving God, certain of the presence of your Holy Spirit,
    we ask you for the gifts of wisdom and understanding,

of knowledge and counsel,
of courage and strength,
of prayerfulness and awe.
Accept the prayer we offer you
in the name of your Son, Jesus Christ.

Reflect on the presence of the Spirit in our lives.

Holy Spirit, we stand firm, here before you,
with our weakness and longing for you.
We are bound to love one another.
Abide, O Spirit of life!

Let peace fill our hearts,
let love fill our minds.
Make us loving disciples of Christ.
May we all be one,
may we all be yours,
Abide, O Spirit of Life!

Pause and ask that we may put the gifts of the Spirit into action in our lives.

May we walk together in justice.
Teach us wisdom, unite all our hearts.
May your grace be here now to guide us.
Abide, O Spirit of Life!

Actions

• Resolve to be strong in the face of temptation.

• Commit yourself to give up watching television shows that ridicule or contradict Christian values.

Close

End your prayer by listening quietly once again to the song "You Have Anointed Me."

Eucharist: The Bread of Life

"To become the eyes and hands of Christ."

Quiet your mind and heart and center on God's presence. Let your whole being enter into prayer.

Invitation to Pray

Christ nourishes us with the bread of life. Let your whole being enter into prayer and begin in the name of the Father, and of the Son, and of the Holy Spirit. Amen.

Prepare Your Heart

Each time we receive communion, we continue and deepen our initiation into Christ. What is this experience like for you? Where and how do you experience Christ's presence? How have you tried to be Christ's presence for others?

If you are with others, share your reflections if you wish. If alone, reflect in silence.

The Word of God

For I received from the Lord what I also handed on to you, that the Lord Jesus on the night when he was betrayed took a loaf of bread, and when he had given thanks, he broke it and said, "This is my body that is for you. Do this in remembrance of me." In the same way he took the cup also, after supper, saying, "This cup is the new covenant in my blood. Do this, as often as you drink it, in remembrance of me." For as often as you eat this bread and drink the cup, you proclaim the Lord's death until he comes. (1 Cor 11:23–26)

REFLECTION

If you are with others, share your reflections if you wish. If alone, reflect in silence, then write notes in the space provided.

▶ What does it mean to you to be the eyes and hands of Christ? What in your life needs to change so that you live this more completely?

▶ In what ways do you offer Christ's life to others?

MEDITATION ON MUSIC

Allow a moment or two for prayerful silence, then listen to or sing along with "The Eyes and Hands of Christ" by Tom Kendzia (track 19 on CD).

Where two or three are gathered in my name
love will be found, life will abound.
By name we are called, from water we are sent:
to become the eyes and hands of Christ.

One we become no longer strangers.
No longer empty or frail.
Filled with the Spirit, every hunger satisfied.
Christ is the center of our lives.

One in the Spirit, one in the Lord.
One in the breaking of the bread.
Life-giving witness of our dying and new life.
Held by the promise in our hands.

Prayer

God of mystery, aware of your great love
> we offer our prayers of gratitude
> and ask for your care.

Pause and thank God for his covenant with us.

Blessed be the Lord God of Israel,
> for he has looked favorably
> on his people and redeemed them.

He has raised up a mighty savior for us
> in the house of his servant David,
> as he spoke through the mouth
> of his holy prophets from of old,
> that we would be saved from our enemies
> and from the hand of all who hate us.

Recall the effects of the covenant, which are realized in the gift of the Eucharist.

By the tender mercy of our God,
> the dawn from on high will break upon us,
> to give light to those in darkness
> and in the shadow of death,
> to guide our feet into the way of peace.

May God bless and keep us, now and always.
We ask this in the name of Jesus. Amen.

Actions

• Resolve to offer the gift of my week at the Sunday liturgy.

• Commit yourself to "go forth to love and serve the Lord" by visiting someone who is homebound.

Close

End your prayer by listening quietly once again to the song "The Eyes and Hands of Christ."

God Offers Unending Forgiveness

"And hold you in the palm of his hand."

Quiet your mind and heart and center on God's presence. Let your whole being enter into prayer.

Invitation to Pray

Our God is the God of holiness! Turn your hearts now to God and begin in the name of the Father, and of the Son, and of the Holy Spirit. Amen.

Prepare Your Heart

We prepare for reconciliation by examining our conscience for sinfulness and failure. How do you make your examination?

If you are with others, share your reflections if you wish. If alone, reflect in silence.

The Word of God

This is the message we have heard from him and proclaim to you, that God is light and in him there is no darkness at all. If we say that we have fellowship with him while we are walking in darkness, we lie and do not do what is true; but if we walk in the light as he himself is in the light, we have fellowship with one another, and the blood of Jesus his Son cleanses us from all sin. If we say that we have no sin, we deceive ourselves, and the truth is not in us. If we confess our sins, he who is faithful and just will forgive us our sins and cleanse us from all unrighteousness. (1 Jn 1:5–10)

Reflection

If you are with others, share your reflections if you wish. If alone, reflect in silence, then write notes in the space provided.

▶ Have you felt yourself held in the palm of God's hand? When?

▶ What most frightens you? How does God console or strengthen you in the face of this fear?

Meditation on Music

Allow a moment or two for prayerful silence, then listen to or sing along with "On Eagle's Wings" by Michael Joncas (track 13 on CD).

You who dwell in the shelter of the Lord,
who abide in his shadow for life,
say to the Lord: "My refuge, my rock in whom I trust!"

And he will raise you up on eagle's wings,
bear you on the breath of dawn,
make you to shine like the sun,
and hold you in the palm of his hand.

You need not fear the terror of the night,
nor the arrow that flies by day;
though thousands fall about you, near you it shall not come.

Text: Based on Psalm 91. Text and music © 1979, OCP Publications. All rights reserved.

Prayer

O merciful God, you call us to conversion and repentance.
Accept our prayer in the name of Jesus.

Pause and reflect on our need for forgiveness.

We ask you, O Lord, to soften any hardened areas in our hearts,
    to grant your mercy and forgiveness
    for the times we have failed
    and turned away from you.

Pause and reflect on Jesus' call to forgive one another.

We pray, Lord Jesus, for the strength to ask forgiveness of others,
    to seek peace in our relationships with others,
    and to forgive those who may have injured us.
May your Spirit fill our hearts with the gifts
    of mercy, love, and peace. Amen.

Actions

• Resolve to make amends to someone you have hurt.

• Commit yourself to seek reconciliation with someone who has offended you.

Close

End your prayer by listening quietly once again to the song "On Eagle's Wings."

God Heals Us through Anointing

"You have anointed me."

Quiet your mind and heart and center on God's presence. Let your whole being enter into prayer.

Invitation to Pray

Our God heals and strengthens us. Turn your hearst to God and begin in the name of the Father, and of the Son, and of the Holy Spirit. Amen.

Prepare Your Heart

The Church blesses and uses holy oils for anointing. Why is this such a powerful gift?

If you are with others, share your reflections if you wish. If alone, reflect in silence.

The Word of God

Are any among you suffering? They should pray. Are any cheerful? They should sing songs of praise. Are any among you sick? They should call for the elders of the Church and have them pray over them, anointing them with oil in the name of the Lord. (Jas 5:13–14)

They had come to hear him and to be healed of their diseases; and those who were troubled with unclean spirits were cured. And all in the crowd were trying to touch him, for power came out from him and healed all of them. (Lk 6:18–19)

Reflection

If you are with others, share your reflections if you wish. If alone, reflect in silence, then write notes in the space provided.

▶ How have you known God's healing touch?

▶ Does someone in your life need to know God's healing love? How can you offer consolation or help?

Meditation on Music

Allow a moment or two for prayerful silence, then listen to or sing along with "You Have Anointed Me" by Mike Balhoff, Gary Daigle, and Darryl Ducote (track 18 on CD).

To bring glad tidings to the lowly, to heal the broken heart,
you have anointed me.
To proclaim liberty to captives, release to prisoners,
you have anointed me.

Your Spirit, O God, is upon me,
you have anointed me.

To announce a year of favor, to comfort those who mourn,
you have anointed me.
To give them the oil of gladness, and share a mantle of joy,
you have anointed me.

Prayer

O loving God, we offer you the prayer of the psalmist
  who expresses confidence in you in time of need.
Accept this prayer from our hearts.

Pause and recall Jesus' parable of the good shepherd.

The Lord is my shepherd, I shall not want.
He makes me lie down in green pastures;
  he leads me beside still waters;
  he restores my soul.
He leads me in right paths for his name's sake.
Even though I walk through the darkest valley,
I fear no evil; for you are with me; your rod and your staff—
  they comfort me.

Pause and pray for God's anointing.

You prepare a table before me
  in the presence of my enemies;
  you anoint my head with oil; my cup overflows.
Surely goodness and mercy shall follow me
  all the days of my life,
  and I shall dwell in the house of the Lord
  my whole life long.

(Ps 23:1–6)

Actions

• Pray today for those who are sick, especially those near death.

• Carry your cross today with patience and peace.

Close

End your prayer by listening quietly once again to the song "You Have Anointed Me."

Consecrated for Service

"Open my eyes, Lord. Help me to see."

Quiet your mind and heart and center on God's presence. Let your whole being enter into prayer.

Invitation to Pray

God calls us to be members of Christ's body. Thanks be to God! Let your whole being enter into prayer, and begin in the name of the Father, and of the Son, and of the Holy Spirit. Amen.

Prepare Your Heart

Christ is the only true priest, and all others are his ministers. How do you see this being lived out by priests whom you know?

If you are with others, share your reflections if you wish. If alone, reflect in silence.

The Word of God

These are the things you must insist on and teach. Let no one despise your youth, but set the believers an example in speech and conduct, in love, in faith, in purity. Until I arrive, give attention to the public reading of scripture, to exhorting, to teaching. Do not neglect the gift that is in you, which was given to you through prophecy with the laying on of hands by the council of elders. Put these things into practice, devote yourself to them, so that all may see your progress. Pay close attention to yourself and to your teaching; continue in these things, for in doing this you will save both yourself and your hearers. (1 Tim 4:11–16)

Reflection

If you are with others, share your reflections if you wish. If alone, reflect in silence, then write notes in the space provided.

▶ How does Christ open your eyes to see the needs of others?

▶ How do you offer service as a sign of your love of Christ?

▶ In what ways have you experienced the "holy order" of the priesthood?

Meditation on Music

Allow a moment or two for prayerful silence, then listen to or sing along with "Open My Eyes, Lord" by Jesse Manibusan (track 20 on CD).

Open my eyes, Lord.
Help me to see your face.
Open my eyes, Lord.
Help me to see.

Open my ears, Lord.
Help me to hear your voice.
Open my ears, Lord.
Help me to hear.

Prayer

Relying on the presence of the Spirit of God with us,
    we pray together:
We stand firm, here before you,
    with our weakness and longing for you.
We are bound to love one another.
Abide, O Spirit of life!

We ask you to guide all our actions
    and to show the path we should walk.
We desire to know what will please you.
Abide, O Spirit of Life!

Pause and pray for light and strength for all those consecrated to the service of the Church.

May you be our sole inspiration,
    may you see whatever we do,
    may we act in your name forever.
Abide, O Spirit of Life!

United in your name forever,
    may our work reflect your desires.
May your mercy and love always fill us.
Abide, O Spirit of Life!

Actions

• Resolve to pray for all ordained ministers of the Church.

• Assist your parish in one of its programs, even if in a small way.

Close

End your prayer by listening quietly once again to the song "Open My Eyes, Lord."

Love Blessed and Celebrated

"Here I am, standing right beside you."

Quiet your mind and heart and center on God's presence. Let your whole being enter into prayer.

INVITATION TO PRAY

Praise Christ who brings us together! Turn your hearts now to God and begin in the name of the Father, and of the Son, and of the Holy Spirit. Amen.

PREPARE YOUR HEART

What is your vocation? How do you fulfill this vocation?

If you are with others, share your reflections if you wish. If alone, reflect in silence.

THE WORD OF GOD

In the same way, husbands should love their wives as they do their own bodies. He who loves his wife loves himself. For no one ever hates his own body, but he nourishes and tenderly cares for it, just as Christ does for the Church, because we are members of his body. For this reason a man will leave his father and mother and be joined to his wife, and the two will become one flesh. This is a great mystery, and I am applying it to Christ and the Church. (Eph 5:28–32)

Reflection

If you are with others, share your reflections if you wish. If alone, reflect in silence, then write notes in the space provided.

▶ How do you experience God's love, waiting for you in the midst of every circumstance?

▶ When has Christ been present in tenderness and mercy in your life? How have you shared this tenderness and mercy with another?

Meditation on Music

Allow a moment or two for prayerful silence, then listen to or sing along with "Here I Am" by Tom Booth (track 21 on CD).

Here I am, standing right beside you.
Here I am; do not be afraid.
Here I am, waiting like a lover.
I am here; here I am.

Do not fear when the tempter calls you.
Do not fear even though you fall.
Do not fear, I have conquered evil.
Do not fear, never be afraid.

I am here in the face of ev'ry child.
I am here in ev'ry warm embrace.
I am here with tenderness and mercy.
Here I am, I am here.

Prayer

Loving God, in marriage a man and woman give themselves
  each to the other to live a covenant of faithful and fruitful love.
Bless all married couples with your grace and the gifts of the Spirit.

Pause and pray for those called to the married life and those who are
already married.

God of love, give strength and happiness
  to all couples who have committed themselves
  to forming an intimate communion of life and love.
May they be of mutual help and comfort to one another,
  and live their marriage vows with fidelity and trust.

Pause and recall the purpose of marriage as ordained by God.

Merciful God, Christian marriage
  is for the good of the couple
  as well as for the generation and education of children.
May Christian homes be communities of grace and prayer,
  and schools of human virtues and of charity.
We pray especially for those
  whose married lives are filled with pain or trial,
  for married couples striving to be
  signs of Christ's love for the Church,
  and for persons whose spouses have died.

Actions

• Resolve to take a step toward making your household "a household of faith."

• Commit yourself to grow in a love that is unconditional.

Close

End your prayer by listening quietly once again to the song "Here I
Am."

Free in the Spirit

"O God, you search me and you know me."

Quiet your mind and heart and center on God's presence. Let your whole being enter into prayer.

Invitation to Pray

Our God is a God of love. Turn your hearts now to God and begin in the name of the Father, and of the Son, and of the Holy Spirit. Amen.

Prepare Your Heart

How does your life reflect your awareness of the dignity of each person?

If you are with others, share your reflections if you wish. If alone, reflect in silence.

The Word of God

When Jesus saw the crowds, he went up the mountain; and after he sat down, his disciples came to him. Then he began to speak, and taught them, saying:
"Blessed are the poor in spirit, for theirs is the kingdom of heaven.
Blessed are those who mourn, for they will be comforted.
Blessed are the meek, for they will inherit the earth.
Blessed are those who hunger and thirst for righteousness,
    for they will be filled.
Blessed are the merciful, for they will receive mercy.

Blessed are the pure in heart, for they will see God.

Blessed are the peacemakers, for they will be called children of God.

Blessed are those who are persecuted for righteousness' sake,
    for theirs is the kingdom of heaven.

Blessed are you when people revile you and persecute you and utter all kinds of evil against you falsely on my account. Rejoice and be glad, for your reward is great in heaven, for in the same way they persecuted the prophets who were before you." (Mt 5:1–12)

Reflection

If you are with others, share your reflections if you wish. If alone, reflect in silence, then write notes in the space provided.

▶ What does freedom mean to you?

▶ Do you have a sense of who you are as a person? How are you responding to that gift?

Meditation on Music

Allow a moment or two for prayerful silence, then listen to or sing along with "O God, You Search Me" by Bernadette Farrell (track 7 on CD).

O God, you search me and you know me.
All my thoughts lie open to your gaze.
When I walk or lie down you are before me:
Ever the maker and keeper of my days.

You know my resting and my rising.
You discern my purpose from afar,
And with love everlasting you besiege me:
In ev'ry moment of life or death, you are.

Text: 99 11 11; based on Psalm 139. Text and music © 1992, Bernadette Farrell. Published by OCP Publications. All rights reserved.

Prayer

Loving God, we are destined to be with you
   and to enjoy eternal happiness.
May we live as your children, following the law
   you have written in our hearts.

Pause and recall the beatitudes Jesus has given us.

Lord Jesus, you have given us the beatitudes
   to help us respond to the desire for happiness
   God has placed in our hearts.
May our lives reflect these teachings
   so we may find true blessedness.

Pause and reflect on the meaning of freedom.

Lord God, you have made us in your image
   and given us the right to exercise freedom.
May our choices always lead us closer to you
   and not lessen our human dignity as your sons and daughters.
We ask this in Jesus' name. Amen.

Actions

• Resolve to let your choices today be directed by the beatitudes.

• Choose at least one way to become involved in a work of social justice.

Close

End your prayer by listening quietly once again to the song "O God, You Search Me."

Making Moral Judgments

"Your life could make us free."

Quiet your mind and heart and center on God's presence. Let your whole being enter into prayer.

Invitation to Pray

Our God is holiness and light! Thanks be to God! Let your whole being enter into prayer and begin in the name of the Father, and of the Son, and of the Holy Spirit. Amen.

Prepare Your Heart

How do you remain open to the challenge of living an upright and truthful life?

If you are with others, share your reflections if you wish. If alone, reflect in silence.

The Word of God

You were taught to put away your former way of life, your old self, corrupt and deluded by its lusts, and to be renewed in the spirit of your minds, and to clothe yourselves with the new self, created according to the likeness of God in true righteousness and holiness. So then, putting away falsehood, let all of us speak the truth to our neighbors, for we are members of one another. (Eph 4:22–25)

REFLECTION

If you are with others, share your reflections if you wish. If alone, reflect in silence, then write notes in the space provided.

▶ Are you lured by things you know are wrong? How do you seek to avoid such temptations?

▶ How does your life reflect Christ's truth and goodness?

MEDITATION ON MUSIC

Allow a moment or two for prayerful silence, then listen to or sing along with "Change Our Hearts" by Rory Cooney (track 9 on CD).

Change our hearts this time, your word says it can be.
Change our minds this time, your life could make us free.
We are the people your call set apart,
Lord, this time change our hearts.

Brought by your hand to the edge of our dreams,
one foot in paradise, one in the waste;
drawn by your promises, still we are lured
by the shadows and the chains we leave behind.

Now as we watch you stretch out your hands,
offering abundances, fullness of joy.
Your milk and honey seem distant, unreal,
when we have bread and water in our hands.

Prayer

Merciful God, we seek your wisdom and guidance.
Accept the psalm-prayer we offer to you,
asking that we may grow in purity of heart.

Pause and recall that Jesus has washed us clean in his blood.

Have mercy on me, O God,
according to your steadfast love;
according to your abundant mercy
blot out my transgressions.
Wash me thoroughly from my iniquity,
and cleanse me from my sin.

*Pause and reflect that God delights more in a contrite heart than in any
sacrifice.*

O Lord, open my lips, and my mouth will declare your praise.
For you have no delight in sacrifice;
if I were to give a burnt offering,
you would not be pleased.
The sacrifice acceptable to God is a broken spirit;
a broken and contrite heart, O God, you will not despise.

(Ps 51:1–2, 15–17)

Actions

• Pray for guidance in making the right choices.

• Read and reflect on one of Jesus' teachings, and let it guide your
choices today.

Close

End your prayer by listening quietly once again to the song "Change
Our Hearts."

The Greatest Virtue Is Love

"May our lives be rooted in love."

Quiet your mind and heart and center on God's presence. Let your whole being enter into prayer.

Invitation to Pray

God calls us to be people of love. Turn your hearts to God and begin in the name of the Father, and of the Son, and of the Holy Spirit. Amen.

Prepare Your Heart

The greatest of all the virtues is charity. Living with charity means treating each and every person we encounter as we would treat Christ himself. How have you done this in the past month?

If you are with others, share your reflections if you wish. If alone, reflect in silence.

The Word of God

As God's chosen ones, holy and beloved, clothe yourselves with compassion, kindness, humility, meekness, and patience. Bear with one another and, if anyone has a complaint against another, forgive each other; just as the Lord has forgiven you, so you also must forgive. Above all, clothe yourselves with love, which binds everything together in perfect harmony. And let the peace of Christ rule in your hearts, to which indeed you were called in the one body. And be thankful. (Col 3:12–15)

REFLECTION

If you are with others, share your reflections if you wish. If alone, reflect in silence, then write notes in the space provided.

▶ How is faith in Christ rooted in your heart? To what does that faith call you?

▶ Is your life filled with the strength of Christ's love? How do you cultivate this presence of Christ in your life?

MEDITATION ON MUSIC

Allow a moment or two for prayerful silence, then listen to or sing along with "Dwelling Place" by John Foley, SJ (track 22 on CD).

I fall on my knees to the Father of Jesus,
the Lord who has shown us the glory of God.

May Christ find a dwelling place of faith in our hearts.
May our lives be rooted in love, rooted in love.

May Christ in his love give us strength for our living,
the strength of the Spirit, the glory of God.

Text based on Ephesians 3. Text and music © 1976, John B. Foley, SJ and OCP Publications. All rights reserved.

PRAYER

God of holiness, may we seek to follow daily in Christ's footsteps,
   growing in the virtues he practiced.
Accept the prayer we carry in our hearts.

Pause and recall the example of Christ.

Confident of Christ's everlasting love, we pray
for compassion and kindness,
for humility, meekness, and patience,
for forgiveness and the willingness to forgive others,
for grateful hearts,
for lives patterned in love.

Pause and thank God for the gifts of grace and virtue.

My soul magnifies the Lord,
and my spirit rejoices in God my Savior,
for he has looked with favor
on the lowliness of his servant.
His mercy is for those who fear him
from generation to generation.
He has shown strength with his arm;
he has scattered the proud in the
thoughts of their hearts.
He has brought down the powerful from their thrones,
and lifted up the lowly.
He has filled the hungry with good things,
and sent the rich away empty.
May God bless us and keep us, now and always. Amen.

Actions

• Decide on a virtue you need to cultivate in your life.

• Reflect on whether there is someone in your life to whom you need to show more love and compassion.

Close

End your prayer by listening quietly once again to the song "Dwelling Place."

Turning Away from God

"A clean heart, O God, create in me."

Quiet your mind and heart and center on God's presence. Let your whole being enter into prayer.

Invitation to Pray

God seeks our living love, and in this love we gather. Turn your hearts to God and begin in the name of the Father, and of the Son, and of the Holy Spirit. Amen.

Prepare Your Heart

We are created with a target in life, and when we sin, we miss that mark. How have you experienced the effects of this in your life? How have you sought reconciliation following such events?

If you are with others, share your reflections if you wish. If alone, reflect in silence.

The Word of God

Then the son said to him, "Father, I have sinned against heaven and before you; I am no longer worthy to be called your son." But the father said to his slaves, "Quickly, bring out a robe—the best one— and put it on his feet. And get the fatted calf and kill it, and let us eat and celebrate; for this son of mine was dead and is alive again; he was lost and is found!" And they began to celebrate. (Lk 15:21–24)

REFLECTION

If you are with others, share your reflections if you wish. If alone, reflect in silence, then write notes in the space provided.

▶ How do you offer forgiveness when you have been hurt?

▶ How do you understand conversion?

MEDITATION ON MUSIC

Allow a moment or two for prayerful silence, then listen to or sing along with "Create in Me" by Tom Kendzia (track 23 on CD).

Create in me a clean heart, O God,
a clean heart, O God, create in me.

O God, in your goodness have mercy on me.
In your compassion wipe out my offense.
Thoroughly wash me from my guilt,
and cleanse me from my sins.

For I acknowledge my offense
and my sin is always before me;
against only you have I sinned,
and done what is evil in your eyes.

Text: Psalm 51:3-6, 12-14, 17. Refrain text © 1969, 1981, ICEL. All rights reserved. Used with permission. Music © 1998, Tom Kendzia. Published by OCP Publications. All rights reserved.

PRAYER

O God of love, you seek out the lost sheep
    and bring them back to the flock.

May we never stray from your love, but if we do,
   give us the grace of conversion and the desire to return to you.

Pause and recall Jesus' love for the sinner.

Sure of Christ's victory over sin and death, we pray
   for those who seek to live as Christ teaches,
   for the grace of conversion for those who have wandered,
   for the wisdom and willingness to imitate the love of Jesus,
   for all who bear the effects of the sin of others,
   for any who are spiritually lost.
We offer this prayer in Jesus' name. Amen.

Pause and ask the help of the Holy Spirit.

Relying on the presence of the Spirit of God with us,
   we pray together.
Let peace fill our hearts,
Let love fill our minds.
Make us loving disciples of Christ.
May we all be one,
   may we all be yours,
Abide, O Spirit of Life!

We ask you to guide all our actions
   and to show the path we should walk.
We desire to know what will please you.
Abide, O Spirit of Life!

ACTIONS

• Show compassion toward someone who has failed you.

• Reflect on what thing or situation is your greatest temptation and resolve to avoid it.

CLOSE

End your prayer by listening quietly once again to the song "Create in Me."

Living as a Community

"One we become, no longer strangers."

Quiet your mind and heart and center on God's presence. Let your whole being enter into prayer.

Invitation to Pray

Called to see the dignity of each person, we gather in God's love. Thanks be to God! Enter now into prayer and begin in the name of the Father, and of the Son, and of the Holy Spirit. Amen.

Prepare Your Heart

How do you serve others? How do you contribute to the common good?

If you are with others, share your reflections if you wish. If alone, reflect in silence.

The Word of God

If then there is any encouragement in Christ, any consolation from love, any sharing in the Spirit, any compassion and sympathy, make my joy complete: be of the same mind, having the same love, being in full accord and of one mind. Do nothing from selfish ambition or conceit, but in humility regard others as better than yourselves. Let each of you look not to your own interests, but to the interests of others. (Phil 2:1–4)

Reflection

If you are with others, share your reflections if you wish. If alone, reflect in silence, then write notes in the space provided.

▶ Am I of one mind with my faith community? How do I show this?

▶ When and how do I look to the interests of others?

Meditation on Music

Allow a moment or two for prayerful silence, then listen to or sing along with "The Eyes and Hands of Christ" by Tom Kendzia (track 19 on CD).

Where two or three are gathered in my name
love will be found, life will abound.
By name we are called, from water we are sent:
to become the eyes and hands of Christ.

One we become, no longer strangers.
No longer empty or frail.
Filled with the Spirit, every hunger satisfied.
Christ is the center of our lives.

One in the Spirit, one in the Lord.
One in the breaking of the bread.
Life-giving witness of our dying and new life.
Held by the promise in our hands.

Prayer

Drawn together by Christ's love, we pray for a society
    built on love and respect for one another.
Lord Jesus, we pray
    for peace and justice,
    for the willingness to put others first,
    for all who serve unselfishly,
    for the poor, the homeless, any who are oppressed.

Pause and ask God that we may be an example of love in our society.

Seeking God's guidance, we pray together.
Be love! O God of goodness!
Look down on us your Church,
    and send the light of grace!

Be love! O Holy Spirit.
Guide us in our decisions,
    hear our prayers.

Be love! O Jesus Christ,
    you save us from all harm
    and lead us to salvation.
May God bless us and keep us, now and always. Amen.

Actions

• Choose one way in which you can be a better neighbor, and act on it.

• Pray for those who suffer from injustice.

Close

End your prayer by listening quietly once again to the song "The Eyes and Hands of Christ."

Sharing God's Life

"Your love and your grace are enough for me."

Quiet your mind and heart and center on God's presence. Let your whole being enter into prayer.

Invitation to Pray

Our God gives us grace and peace. Turn your hearts to God and begin in the name of the Father, and of the Son, and of the Holy Spirit. Amen.

Prepare Your Heart

What does the word "grace" mean to you? Do the life of grace and the vocation to holiness have priority in your daily life?

If you are with others, share your reflections if you wish. If alone, reflect in silence.

The Word of God

Therefore, my beloved, just as you have always obeyed me, not only in my presence, but much more now in my absence, work out your own salvation with fear and trembling; for it is God who is at work in you, enabling you both to will and to work for his good pleasure.

(Phil 2:12–13)

REFLECTION

If you are with others, share your reflections if you wish. If alone, reflect in silence, then write notes in the space provided.

▶ How is God at work in you?

▶ Do you regularly ask God to guide your heart and direct your actions?

MEDITATION ON MUSIC

Allow a moment or two for prayerful silence, then listen to or sing along with "Take, Lord, Receive" by John Foley, SJ (track 24 on CD).

Take, Lord, receive all my liberty,
my memory, understanding, my entire will.

Give me only your love and your grace:
that's enough for me.
Your love and your grace are enough for me.

Take, Lord, receive all I have and possess.
You have given all to me; now I return it.

PRAYER

O loving God, the new law is the grace of the Holy Spirit
    received in your Son, Christ.
May we always live in that grace, heeding the words of the gospel
    and sustained by the sacraments.
Accept this prayer from our hearts.

Pause and reflect that grace makes us God's own children.

Lord Jesus, through your new law, reform our hearts.
Through your Spirit strengthen the virtues
    of faith, hope, and charity in us.
Teach us to forgive others so as to be more like you.

Pause and recall how Jesus prayed for others.

Trusting in you, O God, with our whole heart, we pray
    for the willingness to act on behalf of others,
    for insight and courage,
    for all who ache for love,
    for any who need God's care and our attention.

ACTIONS

• Reflect to see if there is any group or individual whom you look down upon, and resolve to change your attitude.

• Give of your time or material goods to a charitable cause.

CLOSE

End your prayer by listening quietly once again to the song "Take, Lord, Receive."

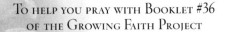

Living with the Mind of Christ

"Bringing God's light to our eyes."

Quiet your mind and heart and center on God's presence. Let your whole being enter into prayer.

Invitation to Pray

The words of the Lord are spirit and life! Turn your hearts now to God and begin in the name of the Father, and of the Son, and of the Holy Spirit. Amen.

Prepare Your Heart

How are the ten commandments and the beatitudes a guide for your life?

If you are with others, share your reflections if you wish. If alone, reflect in silence.

The Word of God

Hear, O Israel: The Lord is our God, the Lord alone. You shall love the Lord your God with all your heart, and with all your soul, and with all your might. Keep these words that I am commanding you today in your heart. Recite them to your children and talk about them when you are at home and when you are away, when you lie down and when you rise. (Deut 6:4–7)

Reflection

If you are with others, share your reflections if you wish. If alone, reflect in silence, then write notes in the space provided.

▶ How are the Lord's words spirit and life for you?

▶ Does the law of love bring you new vision?

▶ Do you put love for God before the things of this world? How?

Meditation on Music

Allow a moment or two for prayerful silence, then listen to or sing along with "Your Words Are Spirit and Life" by Bernadette Farrell (track 4 on CD).

Your words are spirit and life, O Lord:
richer than gold, stronger than death.
Your words are spirit and life, O Lord; life everlasting.

God's precepts keep us; their purpose is right.
They gladden the hearts of people.
God's command is so clear it brings us new vision;
bringing God's light to our eyes.

Living by God's truth is holy and sure;
God's presence is everlasting.
God's truth is eternal, bringing us justice;
bringing God's justice to earth.

Text: Based on Psalm 19:8-11. Text and music © 1993, Bernadette Farrell. Published by OCP Publications. All rights reserved.

Prayer

Lord Jesus, you told the young man,
    "If you wish to be perfect, go, sell your possessions,
    then, come, follow me!"
Let us not hesitate to give up whatever is hindering us
    on the path to perfection.
May we also help others along the way.

Pause and reflect on the Spirit's action in our lives.

Relying on the presence of the Spirit of God with us,
    we pray together:
Let peace fill our hearts,
Let love fill our minds.
Make us loving disciples of Christ.
May we all be one,
    may we all be yours,
Abide, O Spirit of Life!

We ask you to guide all our actions
    and to show the path we should walk.
We desire to know what will please you.
Abide, O Spirit of Life!

Actions

• Reflect on the example of Dorothy Day and of others who have witnessed to justice.

• Discover one thing that is hindering you on the path to holiness and ask God's help to overcome it.

Close

End your prayer by listening quietly once again to the song "Your Words Are Spirit and Life."

We Worship One God

"I, the Lord, am with you."

Quiet your mind and heart and center on God's presence. Let your whole being enter into prayer.

Invitation to Pray

God alone is our creator and Lord. Thanks be to God! Let your whole being enter into prayer and begin in the name of the Father, and of the Son, and of the Holy Spirit. Amen.

Prepare Your Heart

False gods abound in today's world. Among them are the idea that money can buy happiness or make us more secure or create a better life. What are your false gods?

If you are with others, share your reflections if you wish. If alone, reflect in silence.

The Word of God

Jesus said, "Do not store up for yourselves treasures on earth, where moth and rust consume and where thieves break in and steal; but store up for yourselves treasures in heaven, where neither moth nor rust consumes and where thieves do not break in and steal. For where your treasure is, there your heart will be also.

"No one can serve two masters; for a slave will either hate the one and love the other, or be devoted to the one and despise the other. You cannot serve God and wealth." (Mt 6:19–21, 24)

Reflection

If you are with others, share your reflections if you wish. If alone, reflect in silence, then write notes in the space provided.

▶ How does your belief in God affect your daily life?

▶ Where does your treasure lie?

Meditation on Music

Allow a moment or two for prayerful silence, then listen to or sing along with "I, the Lord" by Tom Kendzia (track 16 on CD).

I, the Lord, am with you, always by your side.
Come and take my hand, for I will lead you home.
Follow me, follow me.

I am the resurrection,
and I am the life;
if you believe in me,
you shall live forever.

You shall have new life
and live it to the full.
Turn your sorrow into joy,
for life has just begun.

Prayer

O Lord, our God, we worship you as our creator
    and honor your holy name.
May we never be deceived by the false gods of this world,
    or treat holy things with disrespect.
We ask this in the name of your Son, Jesus.

Brief sacred pause

Placing our trust in you, O God of all, we pray
  for insight in discerning priorities,
  for compassion rather than self-centeredness,
  for commitment to justice,
  for all who seek God,
  for hearts centered on Christ.

Pause to honor God's name in your heart.

Blessed be God!
Blessed be God's holy name!
Blessed be Jesus Christ, true God and true man!
Blessed be the Holy Spirit, the Lord and giver of life!
Blessed be God our Creator!
Blessed be God our Redeemer!
Blessed be God, our Sanctifier!
Blessed be God, the shepherd of our souls!
May God be blessed now and forever!

Actions

• Decide on one way to honor God in your life.
• Resolve to make time for prayer every day.

Close

End your prayer by listening quietly once again to the song "I, the Lord."

We Keep Holy the Lord's Day

"Turn to me, and be saved."

Quiet your mind and heart and center on God's presence. Let your whole being enter into prayer.

Invitation to Pray

Our God is the God of the Sabbath. Thanks be to God! Turn your hearts to God and begin in the name of the Father, and of the Son, and of the Holy Spirit. Amen.

Prepare Your Heart

Nothing we Catholics do is more important than celebrating the Eucharist together. Why is the Mass important to you?

If you are with others, share your reflections if you wish. If alone, reflect in silence.

The Word of God

Remember the Sabbath day, and keep it holy. Six days you shall labor and do all your work. But the seventh day is a Sabbath to the Lord your God; you shall not do any work—you, your son or your daughter, your male or female slave, your livestock, or the alien resident in your towns. For in six days the Lord made heaven and earth, the sea, and all that is in them, but rested the seventh day; therefore the Lord blessed the sabbath day and consecrated it.

(Ex 20:8–11)

Reflection

If you are with others, share your reflections if you wish. If alone, reflect in silence, then write notes in the space provided.

▶ How does keeping Sunday holy enrich your life?

▶ How do you make Sunday a family day?

Meditation on Music

Allow a moment or two for prayerful silence, then listen to or sing along with "Turn to Me" John Foley, SJ (track 2 on CD).

Turn to me, O turn, and be saved,
says the Lord, for I am God;
there is no other, none beside me.
I call your name.

I am God, who comforts you;
Who are you to be afraid of flesh that fades,
is made like the grass of the field, soon to wither.

Listen to me, my people; give ear to me, my nation:
a law will go forth from me,
and my justice for a light to the people.

Text based on Isaiah 45:22-23; 51:12, 4, 6. Text and music © 1975, John B. Foley, SJ and OCP Publications. All rights reserved.

Prayer

Loving God, we honor Sunday as the day on which
    Jesus your Son rose from the dead.
May we keep it holy by observing it
    as a day of rest, of prayer, of family.
Accept the prayer our hearts offer you.

Brief sacred pause

Lord Jesus, we come together on Sunday
    to celebrate your paschal mystery.
We gather in your name and offer you ourselves
    and all we have accomplished during the past week.
Bless our efforts to walk in your footsteps.
May we receive your body and blood with joy and pure hearts.

Pause to rejoice for this holy day.

This is the day that the Lord has made.
Let us be glad and rejoice in it.
Blessed is the one who comes in the name of the Lord.
We bless you from the house of the Lord.
The Lord is God and he has given us light.
Bind the festal procession with branches
    up to the horns of the altar.

(Ps 118:24–27)

Actions

• Resolve to do something special to celebrate this Sunday.

• Invite a guest to share your family meal.

Close

End your prayer by listening quietly once again to the song "Turn to Me."

Forming a Household of faith

"Seek the face of the Lord."

Quiet your mind and heart and center on God's presence. Let your whole being enter into prayer.

Invitation to Pray

Our God is a God of love! Turn your hearts now to God and begin in the name of the Father, and of the Son, and of the Holy Spirit. Amen.

Prepare Your Heart

The life of a family centers around the sharing of the family meal. What role do meals play in your family experience? What are other important times for your family?

If you are with others, share your reflections if you wish. If alone, reflect in silence.

The Word of God

My child, keep your father's commandment, and do not forsake your mother's teaching. Bind them upon your heart always; tie them around your neck. When you walk, they will lead you; when you lie down, they will watch over you; and when you awake, they will talk with you. For the commandment is a lamp and the teaching a light, and the reproofs of discipline are the way of life. (Prov 6:20–24a)

REFLECTION

If you are with others, share your reflections if you wish. If alone, reflect in silence, then write notes in the space provided.

▶ How do you reflect God's everlasting love in your family relationships?

▶ What does being a member of a family or community teach you about God's ways?

▶ How does your family seek the face of the Lord?

MEDITATION ON MUSIC

Allow a moment or two for prayerful silence, then listen to or sing along with "I Have Loved You" by Michael Joncas (track 5 on CD).

I have loved you with an everlasting love,
I have called you and you are mine;
I have loved you with an everlasting love,
I have called you and you are mine.

Seek the face of the Lord and long for him:
he will bring you his light and his peace.

Seek the face of the Lord and long for him:
he will bring you his joy and his hope.

PRAYER

Loving God, may our families always be a reflection
  of your communion of persons, united in love.

We ask that you bless us with peace and harmony.
Accept our prayers as we turn to you.

Reflect that the fourth commandment is rooted in love.

O God, you call us together as a family,
    to be bound to one another in mutual love and respect.
May our families grow as households of faith,
    participating in Christ's own dying and rising
    as we work for the good of one another.

Pause to ask for the fruits of the Holy Spirit.

Lord Jesus, send your Holy Spirit to fill our households
    with the fruits of love, joy, peace, patience, kindness,
    goodness, long-suffering, mildness, faith, modesty,
    continence, and chastity.
We ask this in your name. Amen.

Actions

• Resolve to do a hidden act of kindness for someone in your family.

• Say a prayer for our country and its leaders.

Close

End your prayer by listening quietly once again to the song "I Have Loved You."

Protecting Human Life

"Care for each other, I have cared for you."

Quiet your mind and heart and center on God's presence. Let your whole being enter into prayer.

Invitation to Pray

God of the living, we praise you. Thanks be to God! Let your whole being enter into prayer and begin in the name of the Father, and of the Son, and of the Holy Spirit. Amen.

Prepare Your Heart

How are you called to protect the living?

If you are with others, share your reflections if you wish. If alone, reflect in silence.

The Word of God

See, I have set before you today life and prosperity, death and adversity. If you obey the commandments of the Lord your God that I am commanding you today, by loving the Lord your God, walking in his ways, and observing his commandments, decrees, and ordinances, then you shall live and become numerous, and the Lord your God will bless you in the land that you are entering to possess. But if your heart turns away and you do not hear, but are led astray to bow down to other gods and serve them, I declare to you today that you shall perish; you shall not live long in the land that you are crossing the

Jordan to enter and possess. Choose life so that you and your descendants may live, loving the Lord your God, obeying him, and holding fast to him; for that means life to you and length of days.

(Deut 30:15–20)

Reflection

If you are with others, share your reflections if you wish. If alone, reflect in silence, then write notes in the space provided.

▶ How are you called to love even those whom you do not know?

▶ Has there been a time in your life when the command to respect life moved you to speak out in a difficult or challenging situation? What did you do?

Meditation on Music

Allow a moment or two for prayerful silence, then listen to or sing along with "Love One Another" by Bob Dufford, SJ (track 12 on CD).

Love one another as I have loved you.
Care for each other. I have cared for you.
Bear each other's burdens. Bind each other's wounds;
and so you will know my return.

My friends, do you know what I have done for you?
I have washed your feet with my hands.
If I, your Lord have knelt at your feet,
you should do at each other's feet as I have done for you.

When the world will hate you and revile you,
when they laugh at your care for the poor,
when they hold you in darkness and imprison your tongues,
remember how they listened to me.

Text based on Jn 14-16; 1 Cor 13. Music and text © 1987, Robert J. Dufford, SJ. Published by OCP Publications. All rights reserved.

Prayer

God of life, you created us to respect and care for one another.
May we always defend human life in all its stages,
    and be ready to take a stand when laws threaten innocent life.

Pause and pray for all who work to defend human life.

Created in your image, O God, we now pray
for all who are marginalized
and for all who defend human life:
    for the dignity of all,
    for all who are disabled,
    for those in prison,
    for all who work to preserve and defend life,
    for all who work for peace.
We ask this in the name of your Son, Jesus. Amen.

Actions

• Resolve to take a positive stand on a specific issue threatening human life.

• Make your next gift to someone a contribution in their name to Catholic Relief Services, Heifer International, or another organization that helps the needy.

Close

End your prayer by listening quietly once again to the song "Love One Another."

To help you pray with Booklet #41
of the Growing Faith Project

Called to Chastity

"May Christ in his love give us strength for our living."

Quiet your mind and heart and center on God's presence. Let your whole being enter into prayer.

INVITATION TO PRAY

In Christ, we are called to purity of heart. Let your whole being enter into prayer as we begin in the name of the Father, and of the Son, and of the Holy Spirit. Amen.

PREPARE YOUR HEART

Christian friendship can be a tremendous support. How are your friends a support for you?

If you are with others, share your reflections if you wish. If alone, reflect in silence.

THE WORD OF GOD

So if you have been raised with Christ, seek the things that are above, where Christ is, seated at the right hand of God. Set your minds on things that are above, not on things that are on earth, for you have died, and your life is hidden with Christ in God. Above all, clothe yourselves with love, which binds everything together in perfect harmony.

(Col 3:1–3, 14)

Reflection

If you are with others, share your reflections if you wish. If alone, reflect in silence, then write notes in the space provided.

▶ How does being rooted in love call you to practice modesty and chastity?

▶ How do you respond to influences that are counter to chastity?

Meditation on Music

Allow a moment or two for prayerful silence, then listen to or sing along with "Dwelling Place" by John Foley, SJ (track 22 on CD).

I fall on my knees to the Father of Jesus,
the Lord who has shown us the glory of God.

May Christ find a dwelling place of faith in our hearts.
May our lives be rooted in love, rooted in love.

May Christ in his love give us strength for our living,
the strength of the Spirit, the glory of God.

Text based on Ephesians 3. Text and music © 1976, John B. Foley, SJ and OCP Publications. All rights reserved.

Prayer

Loving God, we ask that we may imitate
  the purity of life of your Son, Jesus Christ.
Fill our minds and hearts with your love.

Pause and reflect on Jesus' promise: "Blessed are the pure in heart, for they will see God" (Mt 5:8).

The Lord is my portion; I promise to keep your words.
I implore your favor with all my heart;
    be gracious to me according to your promise

Pause and recall that God will give us the grace of chastity.

At midnight I rise to praise you,
    because of your righteous ordinances.
I am a companion of all who fear you,
    of those who keep your precepts.
The earth, O Lord, is full of your steadfast love;
    teach me your statutes.

Your hands have made and fashioned me;
    give me understanding
    that I may learn your commandments.
Those who fear you shall see me and rejoice,
    because I have hoped in your word.
I know, O Lord, that your judgments are right,
    and that in faithfulness you have humbled me.

                                        (Ps 119:57–59, 62–64, 73–75)

Actions

• Resolve to put others before yourself today in concrete ways.
• Pray for the gift of chastity.

Close

End your prayer by listening quietly once again to the song "Dwelling Place."

Generosity of Heart

"You have given all to me; now I return it."

Quiet your mind and heart and center on God's presence. Let your whole being enter into prayer.

Invitation to Pray

We praise God who gives us everything. Thanks be to God! Turn your hearts now to God and begin in the name of the Father, and of the Son, and of the Holy Spirit. Amen.

Prepare Your Heart

We imitate Christ when we reach the point of placing spiritual goods over material ones. How are you growing in this quality? What is "enough" for you?

If you are with others, share your reflections if you wish. If alone, reflect in silence.

The Word of God

Then the righteous will answer him, "Lord, when was it that we saw you hungry and gave you food, or thirsty and gave you something to drink? And when was it that we saw you a stranger and welcomed you, or naked and gave you clothing? And when was it that we saw you sick or in prison and visited you?" And the king will answer them, "Truly I tell you, just as you did it to one of the least of these who are members of my family, you did it to me." (Mt 25:37–40)

Reflection

If you are with others, share your reflections if you wish. If alone, reflect in silence, then write notes in the space provided.

▶ In what ways do you say to God, "Take, Lord, receive"?

▶ How and when have you practiced the works of mercy?

Meditation on Music

Allow a moment or two for prayerful silence, then listen to or sing along with "Take, Lord, Receive" by John Foley, SJ (track 24 on CD).

Take, Lord, receive all my liberty,
my memory, understanding, my entire will.

Give me only your love and your grace:
that's enough for me.
Your love and your grace are enough for me.

Take, Lord, receive all I have and possess.
You have given all to me; now I return it.

Prayer

O generous and bountiful God, you call us to share
  the gifts you have given us with our sisters and brothers,
  especially the most needy.
Give us open hands and hearts.
May we never give in to greed of any form.
We ask this in Jesus' name.

Pause and reflect on Jesus' preference for the poor and the outcast of society.

Lord Jesus, may we learn from your example
    to give preference to those
    whom we might tend to neglect or overlook.
For all these and for those of us who can assist them, we pray
    for all who are in need of material assistance,
    for those who are sick and lonely,
    for those who are oppressed and imprisoned,
    for the homeless, the unemployed,
    and those suffering from natural disaster,
    for gracious giving among all believers,
    for all who reach out in selfless service.

May we practice justice and charity in handling
    and managing earthly goods and the fruits of our labor.
May we remember that the goods of creation are destined
    for the entire human race,
    including generations to come. Amen.

Actions

• Resolve that if someone approaches you for help, you will give it.

• Examine how you use natural resources, and choose one area in which you can improve, for example, in the use of water or in recycling.

Close

End your prayer by listening quietly once again to the song "Take, Lord, Receive."

The Truth Makes Us Free

"O God, in your goodness have mercy on me."

Quiet your mind and heart and center on God's presence. Let your whole being enter into prayer.

Invitation to Pray

Christ is our way, life, and truth. Center your whole being on God's presence and begin in the name of the Father, and of the Son, and of the Holy Spirit. Amen.

Prepare Your Heart

The early Christians accepted death rather than lie about their faith. When have you been called to be a witness for truth? What did you do?

If you are with others, share your reflections if you wish. If alone, reflect in silence.

The Word of God

Either make the tree good, and its fruit good; or make the tree bad, and its fruit bad; for the tree is known by its fruit. You brood of vipers! How can you speak good things, when you are evil? For out of the abundance of the heart the mouth speaks. The good person brings good things out of a good treasure, and the evil person brings evil things out of an evil treasure. I tell you, on the day of judgment you will have to give an account for every careless word you utter; for by your words you will be justified, and by your words you will be condemned. (Mt 12:33–37)

Reflection

If you are with others, share your reflections if you wish. If alone, reflect in silence, then write notes in the space provided.

▶ How does the Holy Spirit inspire you to be a person of truth?

▶ In what ways do you witness to the truth?

Meditation on Music

Allow a moment or two for prayerful silence, then listen to or sing along with "Create in Me" by Tom Kendzia (track 23 on CD).

Create in me a clean heart, O God,
a clean heart, O God, create in me.

O God, in your goodness have mercy on me.
In your compassion wipe out my offense.
Thoroughly wash me from my guilt,
and cleanse me from my sins.

For I acknowledge my offense
and my sin is always before me;
against only you have I sinned,
and done what is evil in your eyes.

Prayer

God of truth, give us the gift and courage to speak and act the truth
    especially by witnessing to our faith in our daily lives.
We ask you to accept this prayer which we offer
    in the name of Jesus, your Son.

Recall Jesus' example in speaking the truth.

Lord Jesus, you spoke the truth at all times,
  even when you made enemies among those who did not accept it,
  even when your own disciples couldn't accept it.

Help us be faithful to you and to the message of your gospel.

Pause to pray for the courage to be steadfast and for persons who might suffer for being faithful.

Loving God we ask your guidance in speaking the truth always.
With open hearts, we pray
  for willingness to admit our faults,
  for steadfast spirits,
  for commitment to seek and live in truth,
  for understanding and wisdom,
  for those who bear the weight of mistrust,
  for those who are persecuted for preaching your word.

ACTIONS

• Pray for the courage to witness to the truth.

• Commit yourself to taking action when you see falsehood or a slur against the Catholic faith presented in the media.

CLOSE

End your prayer by listening quietly once again to the song "Create in Me."

Our Relationship with God

"In the shadow of your wings I cling to you."

Quiet your mind and heart and center on God's presence. Let your whole being enter into prayer.

Invitation to Pray

God is always with us as we gather together. Turn your heart now to God and begin in the name of the Father, and of the Son, and of the Holy Spirit.

Prepare Your Heart

Elijah heard God's voice in the sound of "sheer silence." How and when do you hear God's voice?

If you are with others, share your reflections if you wish. If alone, reflect in silence.

The Word of God

The Lord said, "Go out and stand on the mountain before the Lord, for the Lord is about to pass by." Now there was a great wind, so strong that it was splitting mountains and breaking rocks in pieces before the Lord, but the Lord was not in the wind; and after the wind an earthquake, but the Lord was not in the earthquake; and after the earthquake a fire, but the Lord was not in the fire; and after the fire a sound of sheer silence. When Elijah heard it, he wrapped his face in his mantle and went out and stood at the entrance of the cave. (1 Kgs 19:11–13)

Reflection

If you are with others, share your reflections if you wish. If alone, reflect in silence, then write notes in the space provided.

▶ How do you prepare to listen to God?

▶ In what ways do you turn your heart to God in prayer?

Meditation on Music

Allow a moment or two for prayerful silence, then listen to or sing along with "My Soul Is Thirsting" by Steve Angrisano (track 14 on CD).

My soul is thirsting for you, O Lord,
thirsting for you, my God.
My soul is thirsting for you, O Lord,
thirsting for you, my God.
Thirsting for you, my God,
thirsting for you, my God.

O God, you are my God, and I will always praise you.
In the shadow of your wings I cling to you
and you hold me high.

I will never be afraid, for I will not be abandoned.
Even when the road grows long and weary
your love will rescue me.

Prayer

We raise our hearts and our voices to you, merciful God,
offering our gratitude and our needs.

Brief sacred pause

Relying on your presence, O Spirit of God, we pray together.
We stand firm, here before you,
    with our weakness and longing for you.

We are bound to love one another.
Abide, O Spirit of life!
Let peace fill our hearts,
Let love fill our minds.
Make us loving disciples of Christ.
May we all be one,
    may we all be yours,
Abide, O Spirit of Life!

Pause and pray that our actions may reflect our beliefs.

May you be our sole inspiration,
    may you see whatever we do,
    may we act in your name forever.
Abide, O Spirit of Life!
May we walk together in justice.
Teach us wisdom, unite all our hearts.
May your grace be here now to guide us.
Abide, O Spirit of Life!

Actions
- Let your meditation lead to prayer of the heart.
- Use the Liturgy of the Hours for morning or evening prayer.

Close
End your prayer by listening quietly once again to the song "My Soul Is Thirsting."

Jesus Teaches Us to Pray

"Holy Mary, pray for us now."

Quiet your mind and heart and center on God's presence. Let your whole being enter into prayer.

Invitation to Pray

Trusting in God's gracious goodness, we gather together. Turn your hearts now to God and begin in the name of the Father, and of the Son, and of the Holy Spirit. Amen.

Prepare Your Heart

Mary is our model for prayer. She trusted in God completely. Do you trust in God when you pray? How has your life been shaped by such trusting prayer?

If you are with others, share your reflections if you wish. If alone, reflect in silence.

The Word of God

The angel said to Mary, "The Holy Spirit will come upon you, and the power of the Most High will overshadow you; therefore the child to be born will be holy; he will be called Son of God. And now, your relative Elizabeth in her old age has also conceived a son; and this is the sixth month for her who was said to be barren. For nothing will be impossible with God." Then Mary said, "Here am I, the servant of the Lord; let it be with me according to your word." Then the angel departed from her. (Lk 1:35–38)

Reflection

If you are with others, share your reflections if you wish. If alone, reflect in silence, then write notes in the space provided.

▶ In what ways do you say "yes" to God?

▶ How does your life change as a result of your openness in prayer?

Meditation on Music

Allow a moment or two for prayerful silence, then listen to or sing along with "Hail Mary, Gentle Woman" by Carey Landry (track 10 on CD).

Hail Mary, full of grace, the Lord is with you.
Blessed are you among women and blest is the fruit
of your womb, Jesus.
Holy Mary, Mother of God, pray for us sinners now
and at the hour of death. Amen.

Gentle woman, quiet light, morning star, so strong and bright,
gentle Mother, peaceful dove, teach us wisdom; teach us love.

You were chosen by the Father;
you were chosen for the Son.
You were chosen from all women
and for woman, shining one.

Prayer

Loving God, we ask that our prayer
    may always make us open
        to the action of the Spirit, as Mary was.

Pause and reflect on Mary's gratitude to God.

My soul magnifies the Lord,
    and my spirit rejoices in God my Savior,
    for he has looked with favor on
    the lowliness of his servant.
Surely, from now on all generations will call me blessed.
For the Mighty One has done great things for me,
    and holy is his name.

Reflect how Mary finds God acting in the story of salvation.

His mercy is for those who fear him
    from generation to generation.
He has shown strength with his arm;
    he has scattered the proud in the thoughts of their hearts.
He has brought down the powerful from their thrones,
    and lifted up the lowly.
He has filled the hungry with good things,
    and sent the rich away empty.
He has helped his servant Israel,
    in remembrance of his mercy,
    according to the promise he made
    to our ancestors,
    to Abraham and to his descendants forever.

ACTIONS

• Pray especially when you have an important decision to make.

• Resolve to pray even when you do not feel like praying.

CLOSE

End your prayer by listening quietly once again to the song "Hail Mary, Gentle Woman."

God Speaks to Us in Prayer

"I am here with tenderness and mercy."

Quiet your mind and heart and center on God's presence. Let your whole being enter into prayer.

Invitation to Pray

Hearing God's word and holding fast to it, we come together. Center your minds and hearts on God's presence and begin in the name of the Father, and of the Son, and of the Holy Spirit.

Prepare Your Heart

"Work and prayer" was the slogan of St. Benedict. Can you combine work with prayer? How do you fill your daily life with prayer?

If you are with others, share your reflections if you wish. If alone, reflect in silence.

The Word of God

Now the parable is this: The seed is the word of God. The ones on the path are those who have heard; then the devil comes and takes away the word from their hearts, so that they may not believe and be saved. The ones on the rock are those who, when they hear the word, receive it with joy. But these have no root; they believe only for a while and in a time of testing fall away. As for what fell among the thorns, these are the ones who hear; but as they go on their way, they are choked by the cares and riches and pleasures of life, and their fruit does not mature. But as for that in the good soil, these are the ones who, when they hear the word, hold it fast in an honest and good heart, and bear fruit with patient endurance. (Lk 8:11–15)

REFLECTION

If you are with others, share your reflections if you wish. If alone, reflect in silence, then write notes in the space provided.

▶ In what ways is your life filled with praise for God?

▶ How do you receive God's word? What fruits does it bear in your life?

MEDITATION ON MUSIC

Allow a moment or two for prayerful silence, then listen to or sing along with "Here I Am" by Tom Booth (track 21 on CD).

Here I am, standing right beside you.
Here I am; do not be afraid.
Here I am, waiting like a lover.
I am here; here I am.

Do not fear when the tempter calls you.
Do not fear even though you fall.
Do not fear, I have conquered evil.
Do not fear, never be afraid.

I am here in the face of ev'ry child.
I am here in ev'ry warm embrace.
I am here with tenderness and mercy.
Here I am, I am here.

Prayer

Loving God, may we listen to your voice
  as you speak to us in many ways
  during the days and weeks of our lives.
May we call upon you—
  the Source of Life and Divine Love—
  with love and trust.
Accept these prayers which we offer you
  in the name of Jesus your Son.

Pause and offer God praise and thanksgiving.

O come, let us sing to the Lord; let us make a joyful noise
  to the rock of our salvation!
Let us come into his presence with thanksgiving;
  let us make a joyful noise to him with songs of praise!

We pray to our God, the God of creation.

O come, let us worship and bow down,
  let us kneel before the Lord, our Maker!
For he is our God,
  and we are the people of his pasture, and the sheep of his hand.
  (Ps 95:1–7)

Actions

• Take time to center yourself in prayer.

• Make an effort to set aside time each day for prayer.

Close

End your prayer by listening quietly once again to the song "Here I Am."

Becoming Persons of Prayer

"Open my heart, Lord. Help me to love."

Quiet your mind and heart and center on God's presence. Let your whole being enter into prayer.

Invitation to Pray

Our God invites us to grow in prayer. Let your whole being enter into the presence of God and begin in the name of the Father, and of the Son, and of the Holy Spirit. Amen.

Prepare Your Heart

For meditation, all that is required is a quiet place and a quiet heart. Where and when do you find such quiet?

If you are with others, share your reflections if you wish. If alone, reflect in silence.

The Word of God

O Lord, my heart is not lifted up, my eyes are not raised too high;
I do not occupy myself with things too great
    and too marvelous for me.
But I have calmed and quieted my soul,
    like a weaned child with its mother;
        my soul is like the weaned child that is with me.
O Israel, hope in the Lord from this time on and forevermore.

(Ps 131:1–3)

REFLECTION

If you are with others, share your reflections if you wish. If alone, reflect in silence, then write notes in the space provided.

▶ How are your eyes open to God's presence around you?

▶ How are your ears open to the voice of the Lord?

▶ How is your heart open to Christ's love? How do you share that love with others?

MEDITATION ON MUSIC

Allow a moment or two for prayerful silence, then listen to or sing along with "Open My Eyes, Lord" by Jesse Manibusan (track 20 on CD).

Open my eyes, Lord.
Help me to see your face.
Open my eyes, Lord.
Help me to see.

Open my ears, Lord.
Help me to hear your voice.
Open my ears, Lord.
 Help me to hear.

Open my heart, Lord.
Help me to love like you.
Open my heart, Lord.
Help me to love.

Text: Based on Mark 8:22-25. Text and music © 1988, 1998, Jesse Manibusan. Published by spiritand-song.com®. All rights reserved.

PRAYER

Creator God, if we look with eyes of faith,
    we can discover your presence all around us.
Please give us the gift of prayer,
    and help us overcome the difficulties
    that may hinder our growth in you.
We ask this in Jesus' name.

Brief sacred pause

Lord Jesus, teach us to have a prayerful spirit,
    to be one with you and God the Creator and your Spirit.
Teach us to search for you, to focus on you,
    to allow us to be wrapped up in our prayer,
    so we sense the movement of the Spirit
    and live in communion with God.

Reflect that true prayer leads us to act on behalf of others.

Holy Spirit, inspire us to lovingly proclaim the gospel message
    and to live each day by being kind and patient,
    generous and full of love to those around us,
    especially to our sisters and brothers in need. Amen.

ACTIONS

- Lift up the actions of your day to God.
- Resolve to do an act of kindness to someone close to you.

CLOSE

End your prayer by listening quietly once again to the song "Open My Eyes, Lord."

The Lord's Prayer

"Hallowed be thy name."

Quiet your mind and heart and center on God's presence. Let your whole being enter into prayer.

INVITATION TO PRAY

Our God is the God of holiness! Hallowed be God's name! Center on God's presence and begin in the name of the Father, and of the Son, and of the Holy Spirit. Amen.

PREPARE YOUR HEART

We Christians are people of the word of God. How does this affect your life?

If you are with others, share your reflections if you wish. If alone, reflect in silence.

THE WORD OF GOD

Therefore I tell you, do not worry about your life, what you will eat or what you will drink, or about your body, what you will wear. Is not life more than food, and the body more than clothing? Look at the birds of the air; they neither sow nor reap nor gather into barns, and yet your heavenly Father feeds them. Are you not of more value than they? And can any of you by worrying add a single hour to your span of life? And why do you worry about clothing? Consider the lilies of the field, how they grow; they neither toil nor spin, yet I tell you, even Solomon in all his glory was not clothed like one of these. But if God so clothes the grass of the field, which is alive today and tomorrow is thrown into the oven, will he not much more clothe you—you of little faith?   (Mt 6:25–31)

REFLECTION

If you are with others, share your reflections if you wish. If alone, reflect in silence, then write notes in the space provided.

▶ What does the passage above tell you about God?

▶ Which phrase of the Lord's Prayer is the most challenging to you? Why?

▶ Which phrase offers you consolation? Why?

MEDITATION ON MUSIC

Allow a moment or two for prayerful silence, then listen to or sing along with "Lord's Prayer" by Tom Kendzia (track 25 on CD).

Our Father, who art in heaven,
hallowed be thy name;
thy kingdom come;
thy will be done on earth as it is in heaven.
Give us this day our daily bread;
and forgive us our trespasses
as we forgive those who trespass against us;
and lead us not into temptation,
but deliver us from evil. Amen.

Prayer

Loving God, in the prayer which Jesus your Son taught us,
  we pray for your the glory, the sanctification of your name,
  the coming of your kingdom, and the fulfillment of your will.
Accept the prayers we now offer from our hearts.

Pause in silent reflection and praise.

Lord Jesus, in the prayer you taught us we present our wants to God.
We ask that our lives be nourished, healed of sin,
  and made victorious in the struggle of good over evil.

*Pause to offer your own petitions to God. Now slowly and with a reverent
spirit, pray with the words Jesus taught us:*

Our Father, who art in heaven,
  hallowed be thy name;
  thy kingdom come;
  thy will be done on earth as it is in heaven.
Give us this day our daily bread;
  and forgive us our trespasses
  as we forgive those who trespass against us;
  and lead us not into temptation,
  but deliver us from evil. Amen.

Actions

• Meditate on one of the petitions of the Lord's Prayer.

• Resolve to reflect on the day's and week's events to discern God's
will for you.

Close

' your prayer by listening quietly once again to the song "Lord's
"